More Praise for *Waiting to Forget*

"A hauntingly evocative memoir. . . . With this book, which culmi-
nates in a search for her lost son, Moorman has gone straight for that
sorrow and laid it powerfully bare."   —Lisa Shea, *Elle*

"An honest, heartfelt account of one woman's feelings, along with a
look at the mixture of guilt, judgment, and recrimination that cloud
adoptions."   —*Kirkus Reviews*

"[Moorman] has an artist's eye for detail and a pitch-perfect literary
voice."   —*The Oregonian*

"A moving memoir of becoming a mother and then having to give
up her child for adoption. . . . Honest and touching."
                                                  —*Library Journal*

"A probing, powerful memoir."   —*Booklist*

Waiting to Forget

ALSO BY MARGARET MOORMAN

My Sister's Keeper
Light the Lights!

Waiting to Forget

MARGARET MOORMAN

W · W · NORTON & COMPANY

NEW YORK · LONDON

First published as a Norton paperback 1998

The text of this book is composed in Galliard with the display set in Windsor Light Condensed. Composition and manufacturing by The Maple-Vail Book Manufacturing Group. Book design by Marjorie J. Flock.

This book is true, although for the sake of privacy I have changed the names and identifying characteristics of individuals and organizations.

Permission to quote from the following is gratefully acknowledged:

Adopting a Child Today, by Rael Jean Isaac and Joseph Spenser, copyright © 1965 by Harper & Row Publishers, Inc. Copyright renewed 1993 by HarperCollins Publishers, Inc. Reprinted by permission of HarperCollins Publishers, Inc.

You're Our Child: The Adoption Experience, copyright © 1987, by Jerome Smith, Ph.D., and Franklin I. Miroff, by permission of the publisher, Madison Books, Lanham, New York, and London.

The Adoption Triangle, copyright © 1978, 1984 by Arthur D. Sorosky, M.D., Annette Baran, M.S.W., and Reuben Pannor, M.S.W.; by permission of the publisher, Corona Publishing Company, San Antonio.

Giving Away Simone: A Memoir of Daughters, Mothers, Adoption, and Reunion, copyright © 1995 by Jan Waldron, by permission of the publisher, Times Books, New York, a division of Random House, Inc.

The Other Mother, copyright © 1991, by Carol Schaefer, by permission of the publisher, SoHo Press, New York.

Secrets, copyright © 1982, by Sissela Bok; by permission of the publisher, Pantheon Books, New York, a division of Random House, Inc.

Wake Up Little Susie: Single Pregnancy and Race Before Roe V. Wade, copyright © by Rickie Solinger, 1992, by permission of the publisher, Routledge: New York and London.

That Night, copyright © 1987 by Alice McDermott, reprinted by permission of Farrar, Straus & Giroux, Inc., New York.

Wouldn't Take Nothing For My Journey Now, copyright © 1995 by Maya Angelou, reprinted by permission of the publisher, Random House, Inc., New York.

Fortune's Daughter, copyright © 1985 Alice Hoffman, reprinted by permission of the publisher, Ballantine Books, a division of Random House, Inc., New York.

Library of Congress Cataloging-in-Publication Data
Moorman, Margaret.
　　Waiting to forget: a memoir / by Margaret Moorman.
　　　p.　　cm.
　　ISBN 0-393-03967-6
　　1. Moorman, Margaret.　2. Birthmothers—United States—Biography.
　3. Adoption—United States—Psychological aspects—Case studies.
　4. Mother and child—United States—Case studies.　I. Title.
HV874.82.M66A3　1996
362.7'34'092—dc20
[B]　　　　　　　　　　　　　　　　　　　　　　　　　　　95-26588

ISBN 0-393-31783-8 pbk.

W. W. Norton & Company, Inc., 500 Fifth Avenue, New York, N.Y. 10110
http://web.wwnorton.com

W. W. Norton & Company Ltd., 10 Coptic Street, London WC1A 1PU

1 2 3 4 5 6 7 8 9 0

To E.

ACKNOWLEDGMENTS

MICHELLE PATRICK made me write this book. For a long time I said to her and to myself that I was doing it only because I needed the work, thinking of the contract with my publisher. Now I know what kind of work I really needed. Thank you, Shelly.

This is not a book I could have written by myself. Luckily, I didn't have to. There are so many people whose help was essential to me that I wish I could thank them in a format more like an abstract-expressionist painting, with their names drawn all over the page in an arabesque of gratitude.

But if I have to put someone first, it will be Joyce Bahr, leader of the Manhattan Birthparents Group, whose balanced, gentle guidance, optimism, fairmindedness, and constant reassurance kept me going.

Katherine Koberg read the first draft and sent it back with nearly 200 Post-it notes bearing advice, every bit of which I tried to heed. Her humor and sensitivity saved me at a critical moment.

I thank my editor, Jill Bialosky, wholeheartedly, for her steadfastness, even more than for the sixty-five pages of cuts.

Beth Vesel, my agent, is my ideal—understanding, thoughtful, and analytical. A calming force.

Thanks to Aly Abrams, Jill Bonamusa, Jill Clark, John Fairfield, Jaymie Friedman Fredericks, Fiona Graham, Trenie Hauser, Paula Heisen, April Kinser, Susan Lemagie, Shellee Rudner, Nancy Traver, and all the friends who encouraged me; to the birth parents, adopted persons, and adoptive parents who shared their insights; to the authors of books through which I gained perspective on my experiences, especially Jean A. S. Strauss, Linda Cannon Burgess, Jan Waldron, and Carol Schaefer.

Many thanks to Alan Cote, for the title.

To A.A., with gratitude.

To M., and to his family.

Last, but most, with love to Harvey.

Waiting to Forget

In all self-revelation, still one other listens and seeks to penetrate the secret regions being explored. This other is the speaker himself.

Sissela Bok, *Secrets*

PROLOGUE

Two little ducks went out to play
Over the hills and far away.
Mother duck said, Quack, quack, quack, quack,
But only one little duck came back.

Children's counting song

1992

AT THE TENDER AGE of forty-four, I have received my first
Mother's Day presents—a brightly-colored papier-mâché
bracelet and four baggies of pastel bath salts: pink, yellow,
blue, and green. The bracelet is gorgeous, the bath salts perfumed.
Laura, three-and-a-half, can see what a hit she's made with these
treasures, and she's proud. Life is luxurious! Life is good.

Later on this hot spring day, watching her play outside with her
father, I'm struck by how much she resembles my side of the family,
at least for now. She used to look so much like my husband that he
once bought her a licorice pipe to mimic his pacifier of choice and
complete the image. It's clear, now, that she also takes after my
grandmother Eva, a beautiful woman, born just after the Civil War,
with large, light eyes tilted up slightly at their outer corners. Eva was
the mother of my father, Bob, dead thirty years now, and of my
favorite relative, my Aunt Ginny, who has been gone since 1986. I
miss that side of my family, and I take great pleasure in seeing their
genetic legacy, passed down from the last century, in my daughter. I
keep that to myself, though, for Laura would be the apple of my eye
no matter how she looked, no matter who she was.

I was forty when, by some miracle of volition and reception, I
became pregnant. When it was time for amniocentesis, I went to

Mount Sinai Hospital for my pre-amnio interview.

The woman seated across a desk from me asked the routine questions—my age, date of birth, medical history. I answered, she wrote, it went along quickly.

And then, still routinely, she asked, "Any previous pregnancies?"

"Yes," I answered readily, but with a slight contraction of spirit.

"How many?"

"One."

"Result?"

"What?"

"Did you miscarry, have an abortion, or carry to term?"

"Carried to term."

"Date?"

"January 15, 1965."

End of routine. The interviewer looked up, stared for a moment beneath arched brows, and then blessed me with a smile. "Wow! Almost a quarter of a century!"

I was off-balance but managed to smile back. I hadn't forgotten that other pregnancy, but the pure joy of this one, rather than reminding me of the first, seemed to have buried it deeper in the past. This pregnancy was a different experience entirely. No morning sickness this time, no afternoon fainting spells. But especially no drymouthed panic. Just bliss, augmented by happy hormones coursing through my body.

As I had approached the age of forty, I had come to feel that motherhood was beyond my reach. My first child, certainly, was beyond my reach, for though he had been a healthy baby boy, I hadn't been his mother. I had been only what has come to be called a birth mother, the mother who gave birth to a child who was adopted.

Now, seeing my daughter grow and develop, the reality of my first child's existence is almost palpable. I do not have even an image of my son's childhood. No pictures, and certainly no memories. I never laid eyes on that baby. I had only a glimpse of a little loaf of blanket in a hospital bassinet, across a room.

With my daughter, I can summon up remembrance of certain moments when she was twelve weeks old and had an expression, for a while, that was so like one of my mother's wry looks that a family friend, on glimpsing it for the nanosecond that was its usual duration, gasped, "That was Sara!" She gasped because Sara, my mother, was not long dead, and to see her intelligent, animated face again was like a peek into the afterlife, or possibly a glance back at the lingering past. I would like to have such a memory of my first baby, and as I write that I answer myself with rueful finality: Not even in your dreams.

For more than two decades I was careful not to disturb the part of my heart that will always grieve for letting my first baby go, but now I am less careful. The happiness I find in mothering my daughter makes it bearable to open up that old wound, the one that never really healed.

As my daughter slipped out of my womb and into the perilous world, I asked my obstetrician, "Do you have to cut the cord?"

"Only literally," was her ready reply.

Jokes have a short shelf-life, though. It's time to examine how losing the first has affected the way I mother the second. During these first few years I've noticed how loath I am to be away from my little girl. Is it just that I'm old enough to know how to savor this blessing? Or am I afraid that if I blink she will be out of my sight forever? There is work to be done here, as the therapists say.

Some children have a finely-tuned sense of the poignance of their situation. One day, out of the blue, as the most important subjects always seem to emerge, Laura said, "I don't want to be a mommy."

"Really?" I answered. "I *love* being a mommy."

She shook her head. "I want to stay your little baby."

I reassured her, telling her that she would always be my baby, forever and ever, but she wouldn't be budged.

"No," she said sadly. "I mean *really*."

I wonder if my first child ever wanted to be mine *really*, instead of only biologically. For his sake, I hope not.

Adoption has been in the news. The DeBoer-Schmidt custody case, in which a child widely called Baby Jessica was returned to her birth parents when she was nearly three years old, caused a furor. People couldn't stop talking about what it all meant. The child's birth mother, Cara Schmidt, was demonized in the popular press, and I found it hard to read the endless editorials and letters to the editor castigating her for changing her mind about relinquishing her baby. I never saw one that emphasized what to me were the salient points of the case: that Cara Schmidt's daughter was born February 8th, 1991; twenty-six days later Cara filed a motion to restore her parental rights; that a judge had instructed the DeBoers, who hoped to become Jessica's adoptive parents, to return the baby to her birth father when she was less than a year old; and that the DeBoers' refusal had stretched the legal battle out until Jessica (or Anna, as her birth parents call her) was old enough to be traumatized by the move.

Painful as it was, the case fired my imagination, forcing me to think, to remember, and to realize that I was not an objective party to any debate about adoption. Looking through a copy of *The New Yorker* that appeared in my mailbox within a couple of weeks of my first complete Mother's Day, I stopped turning pages when I saw the headline "Adoption Country." In an unsigned editorial, a writer proposed that "metaphorically, at least, adoption is what made America great, for America's very nationhood is adoptive. The vast migrations that populated this continent, the uprootings and re-plantings and recombinings of people and peoples (sometimes in sorrow, sometimes in hope) that, far more than ties of biological kinship, created the American nation, can be seen as a historical experiment in mass geographical adoption."

I found myself distracted by stray thoughts of Native Americans and African-Americans—I wondered what they would have to say about, say, the "sorrow" part, considering the brutal nature of their uprootings and replantings. I thought about the ugly prejudice against Italian-Americans, Irish-Americans, and other newcomers before they, too, were accepted into the "family." Besides being inapt, the metaphor seemed inappropriately broad. But then I forced myself to read the article more carefully.

At one point the writer acknowledged that there was "new understanding of the importance of genetic factors in human personality and health," and further that this "may be giving new zeal to groups such as Concerned United Birthparents, many of whose members view adoption, especially confidential adoption, as a kind of class exploitation that results in genealogical trauma." The writer went on. "(Maybe so, but if that's always the case, then Jim Palmer has been traumatized into baseball's Hall of Fame, James Michener has been repeatedly traumatized to the top of the best-seller lists, and Steven Jobs has been traumatized into revolutionizing the computer industry.)"

But who ever said adoption *always* resulted in trauma? I found myself asking the air. I was surprised at the vehemence of my reaction. I recoiled; I practically gaped at the words on the page.

Toward the end of the editorial, the writer cited recent studies showing " 'no significant disadvantages of adoptive as opposed to biologic parenting, and some significant advantages.' (This finding [he wrote] is perfectly consonant with common sense, inasmuch as adoptive parents are always, by definition, parents by choice.)" His implication seemed to be that chosen children have at least that particular advantage over the suprises of biological familyhood.

The thought that chosen children therefore must be doubly loved is one that has comforted me over the years. I have clung to the hope that my son's mother and father regarded his arrival as nothing short of a miracle and that as he grew he remained someone they would choose again and again, if it were possible. But when I read *The New Yorker* writer's similarly hopeful words, I suddenly thought of little Lisa Steinberg, the six-year-old New York City adoptee who had been beaten by her "adoptive" father, Joel Steinberg (the adoption was never legal), and left to die on a bathroom floor while he and the "adoptive" mother, Hedda Nussbaum, who together had reared the child from her birth, took drugs in the next room. And when reading the author's list of successful adoptees, I found myself thinking that Son of Sam might lead a list representing the opposite pole of possibility.

I can almost always avoid such black thoughts—birth parents will do anything to avoid them—except when I'm confronted by someone with a determinedly uncomplicated view of an extremely complicated situation. If the author had acknowledged that adoptive parents and adopted children are capable of the same range of human behaviors and feelings, both positive and negative, as biological parents and children, I doubt I'd have reacted at all. But it seemed obvious to me that being adopted didn't necessarily mean a child was wanted for the right reasons or that she would grow up happy and successful—any more than being a natural offspring ensures that. I know one or two planned, biological children who are, in my view, neglected, and I would not kid myself that the same thing couldn't happen to an adopted child.

My son may be a major-league success—that is a possibility—but one problem for birth parents of my generation is that we seldom know how our babies fared. And while we try to hold on to the image of our children as treasured and well-brought-up, satisfied with their lives and grateful for our sacrifices, we are not always able to make the stretch. We read the papers. We listen to the evening news.

The author of "Adoption Country" mentioned that birth mothers were increasingly demanding "greater and greater openness." He called this one of the "vexing trends" in adoption. It seemed to me to be natural, normal, reasonable, and indicative of their love that birth mothers would demand openness. It also might be said to demonstrate their awareness of the serious nature of the gift they were giving. I wish I had invented open adoption.

When the editors of a news magazine where I worked in the early eighties decided to run a story on adoption, I was sent to report on a group in New York called the Adoptees' Liberty Movement Association, or ALMA. Started by Florence Fisher, an adoptee who searched for, and eventually found, her original parents, ALMA runs a registry for birth families and adoptees who are hoping to reunite.

At the magazine, I revealed my past to the head writer on the project, a woman who, with her husband, had tried unsuccessfully and at great expense to conceive a child and who also had been rejected as adopters by one of the best-known adoption agencies in New York. I was kept on the job despite my confession, my predictable biases perhaps regarded as negligible when compared with her own.

I had strong but mixed emotions when I interviewed Fisher. I still felt, then, that it was important for me not to look back. Not looking back was my only hope of avoiding the guilt, embarrassment, and longing that were wrapped up in memories of my earlier life.

Fisher introduced herself and talked for a while about reunions facilitated by ALMA. She showed me photographs of families who had searched for and found one another, and she read from testimonial letters. She spoke resentfully of her own unhappy childhood and the poor fit she and her adoptive parents had made with one another. She talked about her relief when after decades of searching she found her birth parents, while candidly acknowledging that the results of her search were not all she'd hoped for.

Finally, Fisher pointed at rows upon rows of tall file cabinets that filled a large room and asked rhetorically, "You know what's in those files?"

I waited.

"Pain," she said firmly. "*Pain.* That's what's in those files."

I knew exactly what she meant. My own was an amalgam of sadnesses both large and small. A few weeks before the interview, as I was heading home from work late one evening, I had seen a perfect 1965 Mustang painted, or preserved, in that original knockout color somewhere between vermillion and cadmium red light. I'd had to steady myself against the glass wall of the bus shelter where I was standing. Twenty years earlier, looking down from a pretty yellow bedroom in the warm house where I was hidden away during the long months of my pregnancy, big in the belly, with only a few weeks to go before the birth, I had watched the new Mustang cross a small bridge and turn my way. I was aware of cars, then, and I'd seen magazine ads and television commercials that made it clear to me that this new one was going to be something special, like the Thunderbird, that the kind of boys I grew up with would covet. I was sixteen, and as I looked down on that gorgeous car it seemed to me even then to stand for all the frivolous parts of teenage life from which I had become estranged. Two decades later the same sight made me slightly dizzy with remembered resignation.

There was work to be done there. It was easier for me, then, to turn away from that much pain. Now, I am less reluctant to shine the light of recollection on my memories, anguished as many of them are.

And now, too, I think about my daughter, growing up not only in her own small family but also in a country where the religious and political right threatens to establish a new age of shame, as reproductive freedoms taken for granted for only a short while are now being abridged and denied and legislated away. The last such time, an era of secrets and pain and lies and hypocrisy, wasn't really so long ago. Times are always desperate for pregnant fifteen-year-olds.

My friend Susan, an obstetrician, tells me that most of the unmarried teenagers and young women she treats these days are keeping their babies. I envy them, but I can't help wondering how they will negotiate the difficult years ahead. Motherhood is not even a minimum-wage job. Even with money, even with maturity, it is always hard to be a single parent. But then I consider the alternative. Is it any easier for a woman to carry a baby inside her, give birth, and say goodbye?

As I began to sift through my thoughts, in order to write about them, I found myself afraid of what I might call the room, perpetually

dark to me, for which I do not have the key. The mysterious room
that contains that baby, now nearly thirty.

How much of him is like me, how much like his birth father?
What have the years and his parents made of him, and what has he
made of himself? Is there something about him that is of my line, of
my side of the family, of me? In the Kentucky town of Leitchfield
where my father's family came from, the minister used to say that
you could always tell the Moormans in the congregation Sunday
mornings, because they were the ones with tears streaming down
their cheeks. I wondered if my son inherited that sentimental temper-
ament.

Has he suffered the way my side, at least my father's, seems to
suffer? The Moormans, like many families, have carried a burdensome share of serious illness and of loss, including the early deaths of
many children.

Is he alive?

I could tell that if I wasn't very careful I would work myself into
knots. Maybe my son escaped the family curse (not that I believe in
such things as curses) by being skipped into a new family altogether.
Now, there's a calming thought.

Would I ever know, or be brave enough to try to know?

Marjorie Lane   September 28, 1994
The Winnicott Foundation
4123 Wheaton Road
Springfield, Maryland 30114

Dear Ms. Lane:
    I gave birth to a boy on January 30, 1965, who was adopted
through Winnicott. I am writing you now with a four-part request.
    First, I would like to petition to know where his adoption
was finalized. Please send me any necessary forms.
    Second, I would like to receive copies of any documents rel-
evant to his adoption. I understand that I am entitled to papers
that I signed, and I would also be grateful for any assessments
of me by your social worker that might throw some light on
my state of mind at the time.

Third, my sister, who had already had one psychiatric breakdown by 1965, has been hospitalized more than 25 times since. She has been relatively stable in recent years, but her disease has been debilitating and her life very hard. Could you possibly find out if the son I relinquished has escaped this affliction?

Finally, many, many years ago, I called Winnicott to ask that a note be put in my file saying that I was available to my son or his parents if needed. I was told that it would be illegal for Winnicott to give them my name, even with my consent. I understand that it is now possible to sign a Waiver of Confidentiality, and I would appreciate receiving such a form.

I hope to hear from you soon.

> Sincerely,
> Margaret Moorman

And then, in afterthought, written by hand across the bottom: "I have tried, twice, to get in touch with your predecessor and never received a response. I hope to hear from you in a timely fashion."

PART ONE

One Goodbye After Another

1

Pain has an Element of blank—
It cannot recollect
When it begun—or if there were
A time when it was not—

Emily Dickinson

A‍T FIVE-FOOT-SIX INCHES tall, I had weighed 117 pounds and worn a size 8 since I was twelve, but the summer I turned fifteen, I found I could wear a size 6 Villager shirtwaist without even holding my stomach in.

I didn't throw up every day. There was even a whole week, now and then, when everything stayed down. But I began to come to dinner with a measure of dread, for often enough, I had to run from the table to the toilet.

I was suffering from loss, simple as that, and before long, my body had made itself into a metaphor. No one noticed, or if they did they didn't question me about my inner state. No one asked, no one took me to a doctor, and although I hated throwing up I didn't mind being thin.

My parents were understandably distracted. My older sister, Sally, had returned from an 18-month stay in a mental hospital not long before, and although she was well enough eventually to attend college nearby, her illness required vigilance. At first, she moved into a dormitory, but she soon retreated from the dual strain of independence and group living and moved back home. Home was a difficult place, where fights broke out constantly, and Sally often retreated, spending long hours alone in her room, resting. When she was in her room, my parents fought about whether or not to urge her to come out. When Sally was out, she fought with my mother. If Sally tried to engage me in conversation, I ignored her, wishing that she would return to the hospital and that the house would become quiet again, disturbed only by my parents' worried but at least sub-dued conversations about money.

Since Sally's return, I had managed easily to stay out of that house. I went across the street, to my best friend Louise's, where I commiserated with her on the birth of another brother, which tipped the sibling scale in her family three-to-two. Or I went around the corner to Karen's, where I played with her baby sister. Or to Sharon's. But Sharon, who was a year older than I was, had already entered the frighteningly sophisticated world of high school. Or to Aly's, where I'd stayed many weekends while my parents had visited Sally in the hospital. To Beth's, or Suzy's. Louise, Karen, Aly, Beth, and Suzy were my companions, friends I saw every day, with whom I walked in the woods, did homework, and whispered in class.

We lived in an old part of Arlington, Virginia, across the Poto-mac from Washington, D.C., and I think we were less sophisticated than some of our counterparts in other neighborhoods. We still played in the woods and the creek, we walked to the Methodist church up the street, where we sang in the choir, and we danced in each other's basement rec rooms in the soft glow of blue lightbulbs, surreptitiously placed in the lamps while our parents sat upstairs watching Hit Parade or the Steve Allen Show.

Most of my friends were in military families. Arrivals and depar-tures were common in Arlington, a bedroom community for the Pentagon. Colonels and captains, with their wives and children, came and went and returned and left again, and it wasn't until quite recently, when a childhood friend remarked on the changeableness of our neighborhood, that I realized how unusual it had been.

It was not common for all of my closest friends to move at once, but that is what happened in the summer of 1963. Suzy was the first. The night before her departure we had a slumber party in her basement. Until four or five in the morning, we talked, pledging to write and always to remember and to be friends forever. The next day, when it was time to wave goodbye to her station wagon as her father maneuvered it out of their driveway, it was easy to cry, if only from fatigue.

Louise was the last. I went to National Airport and watched her plane take off for Germany. Beth and Karen had also moved away, Aly had left for a private boarding school, and Sharon was always with her boyfriend. I waved and shielded my eyes as Louise's plane ascended. I stood quite still, so struck by my sudden solitude, my extreme loneliness, that tears were beside the point.

I was alone, too, in another way. Ever since I could remember, I'd had one boyfriend or another, but suddenly I was without. By the age of fifteen, I had a romantic history. I was tall for my age, physically mature at twelve, and older boys were interested in me. Two years earlier, my mother had abetted my involvement with one of them, a lifeguard we'd met on vacation in southern Virginia who'd entered college the following fall, when I went into eighth grade. This boy's interest in me was both flattering and burdensome. I felt stupid and childish around him. Were it not for my mother's attention, the flirtation would have gone the way of the summer.

Decades later, when Judy Blume's books for pre-teens were making a splash, my mother suggested I try to write one of my own. "You could write about a mother who flirts with a college boy and keeps him around by encouraging her young daughter to go out with him," she said.

I gaped at her.

"Well," she said with a shrug, "It might help somebody else."

At thirteen, I had dutifully kept inviting the college boy to visit and sending him joke greeting cards, which my mother bought for that purpose. "Here's a cute one for Frank," she would say, reaching into her purse. "Do you need a stamp?" There was one that said on the front, "It never writes, it never calls: What is it?" Inside there was a hand drawn with its finger pointing at the recipient. I sent it off without thinking, as I was beginning to do everything. Frank sent back a furious letter, reminding me indignantly of his two to three letters a week and his frequent calls.

"Well, *I* haven't heard from him in ages," my mother said when I read her his bitter reply.

Eventually—when I was fourteen and beginning ninth grade—I found someone my own age whom I began meeting at church sock hops and school dances. We kissed at parties, but mostly we were friends. Joe was a gifted artist, who had won thousands of dollars in scholarship money in national design competitions. In shop class he made me a ring that was simple and elegant and turned my finger green.

Impressive though his talents were, it was his silliness that I found irresistible. I was a sucker for someone who could make me laugh. I was also relieved to be rid of sexual pressures. Joe seemed to have none of what Frank, the college boy, called "needs." Joe allowed me to reenter my peer group, making a kind of return to Eden that I would try to repeat many times in my life.

At Frank's last visit, I showed him a school picture of Joe. "This is my boyfriend," I said proudly.

"Then who am I?" Frank asked reasonably but in a tight, rising voice. I was speechless.

Every night I waited by the phone for my sweetheart's telephone call. I bought him small gifts, and wrote him notes, ignoring my father's warning not to "squeeze that puppydog too hard." When Joe broke up with me, he did it the way any very young man would. He asked for his ring back and never spoke to me again.

Losing him was a sign that I could not pretend to fit in. I was already skewed from the norm, trying to undo the effects of too much, too soon with the older boy (to think that in 1963 some modest petting seemed shamefully far to go!), and trying hardest to pretend that my life, unlike my sister's, was one fine day after another.

After a couple of months, I began to eat normally again, but every night, as I lay down to sleep, I would feel hot tears pouring down my cheeks and into my pillow. My chest heaved with deep sighs as I literally cried myself to sleep.

I was bereft, and bereft of hope, in a way I could not have explained, but I was not asked to try.

One chilly, lonely night in the fall of 1963, I picked up a razor from my dresser, removed the blade, and made some shallow, exploratory slices across my left wrist. I was so shocked at the first slow leak of blood that I ran into my parents' bedroom and woke them up. "I cut my wrist," I said matter-of-factly. After I was patched up—taken to an emergency room far from our neighborhood, so that no one we knew would find out about this new trouble in our home—I was asked by my mother if I would like to talk to my sister's psychiatrist. I considered my choices, as I saw them: be like my sister or pull myself together.

"I'm fine," I said.

"Are you sure, Honey?" my mother asked. Then, "Don't you want to wear a long-sleeved blouse, just until the bandages come off?"

Soon after my visible wounds had healed, a boy I knew from church began showing interest in me. He was two years older than I was, but I hardly knew him. His navy family had not been in the neighborhood long, and I had only just entered high school, where he was a senior. We held hands in church; we went out on Friday nights.

I began to feel better in small ways that counted, but on New Year's Eve, 1963, after the calmest Christmas anyone in my often unhappy family could remember, my father died of a heart attack. He fell from a high stool where he sat at his workbench in the utility room, polishing shoes. Our spaniel began barking with a ferocity I had never heard before. I ran from my room, where I had been dressing to go out, and found my father sprawled awkwardly by the furnace. His glasses had flown off and lay nearby, broken. He was unconscious, but he seemed to be struggling to breathe. He stopped gasping. I placed my hand on his chest, to try to feel a heartbeat. A loud, convulsive shudder shook his body. I ran to the telephone and called for an ambulance. Then I covered my father and waited. His face began to turn purple. Because my touch had caused the last, utterly terrifying sound that came from him, I thought I might have killed him. When CPR was developed and publicized a decade later, I finally understood that the pressure of my hand on his chest might have revived him for a moment.

I have often tried to remember where my mother and sister were as I was tearing from room to room. In my mind's eye, I see them standing stock still. Later, my mother accompanied my father's body to the hospital in the ambulance. Neighbors had gathered in the house. When I turned toward a friend of my mother's, my knees buckled under me. That night, lying in my bed in the dark, I decided that I would have to be not just strong, but, as I put it to myself, "the strong one."

Looking back, I see that my psychological resources were already stretched beyond their limit. My sister, on the other hand, rallied coping mechanisms she had learned during her hospital stay. She kept up with her college classes, and she began helping out around the house. Mother, after a period of silent grief, during which she became frighteningly thin—she too was now suffering from loss—eventually went to work at a branch of the county library. No one mentioned my father. No one mentioned his death. I hadn't talked to my sister in years; my mother and sister barely spoke to each other. My mother now went through her days without ever looking my way, with one exception. She took my father's garnet ring, which had been handed down to him by his favorite forebear, his grandfather Papaw, and had it cut down to fit my finger. "I know Daddy would want you to have it," she said. This loving, meaningful gesture blossomed in my mind to stand for whatever hope I could muster. Life *could* go on, though it remained bleakly empty.

Twenty-five years later, my mother would say in a thoughtful, discovering tone, "Daddy's death must have been a shock for you and Sally, too."

Sally and I were called upon to do much of the work around the house after Mother took the library job. I was assigned to making

dinners on week nights. My grief lay where I had buried it. I instinctively knew that the best way for me to keep it in its place was to make
myself busy, to be physically involved in some activity that took my
mind off the troubles in my heart.

One of the most engrossing ways I found to be involved was to
neck for countless hours with my boyfriend in the back seat of his
family's car. I didn't mind his tentative advances the way I'd dreaded
Frank's. There was an innocence to everything Dan did; in sex, I was
the more experienced one. I had lain next to a boy, if not naked at
least aware of the stick of dynamite hidden beneath whatever clothes
separated us. That made me about as experienced as anyone, I figured. One night, as we were parked on a dirt road in a woods about
200 yards from my house, I broke out of a heated kiss and told my
boyfriend that I wanted to tell him something. I was preoccupied
that night—I think about my French teacher, who seemed positively
to hate me—but Dan shook his head and put his finger on my lips.
"It's alright," he said. "I know you're not a virgin."

I was affronted, but I did not argue with him. I felt so haggard at
fifteen that Dan's assumption actually made sense to me. That night
I let him touch me as long as he wanted, wherever he wanted, and I
was grateful that he wanted. And the sensations, to tell the truth,
were wonderful—the heat we generated in the cold car; the breathing that put oxygen in my veins; the tropic turning of every cell of
mine toward every cell of his. It was a pleasure.

Later, in the spring, we decided to try intercourse. We planned
which night and stopped at a restaurant on Lee Highway, where
Dan had seen condom machines in the men's room once. He strode
in nervously, with long, purposeful steps, while I sat in the car,
waiting. I didn't know if one could buy condoms in drug stores,
then, and Dan didn't know, either. I wasn't really sure what a condom was, actually, but I knew it was "birth control." When Dan
came out he shook his head. "No machine," he said.

Birth control was a subject that had been covered, of late, in the
only magazines I read: *Time* and *The Saturday Evening Post*. There
was much discussion of the rhythm method, which I knew was

practiced by Roman Catholics. I knew that an egg was most likely to be fertilized on the fourteenth day of a woman's cycle, and so I added up the days since my last period. I forgot that one counted from the *first* day of a menstrual period, however. I counted from the last. One, two, three, four, five, six—only day six, wasn't that perfectly safe?

Dan backed the car out of the parking spot, and we drove to a woods that I can still picture, still smell—the rotting oak leaves, slightly damp, under the rough, old blanket we'd brought with us. It was April 23, a warm night in northern Virginia in 1964. Or do I only think that because the twenty-third was my friend Aly's birthday? Maybe it was April 16. That date sticks in my mind, too. Later I would be able to look at a calendar and narrow it down to one of two Saturday nights—one of two weekend date nights—in the early spring.

It was with a sense of occasion that we spread out the blanket and lay down on it. It was with exaggerated care that we removed our clothes—all of them, for the first time. And it was with a sense of reverence that we moved together.

We broke apart and lay quietly on our sides in the dark.

By the time we left the woods, clinging to each other in awed, sticky silence, the sperm and egg that were to become someone else's child were on their way to fertilization.

Dan drove me home. I felt quietly happy. Peaceful. At fifteen, I had been more than ready for what happened that night. I have to admit that, awkward as it may have been, I felt no guilt, disappointment, or regret. Those feelings came later.

It took me a long time to understand that I was pregnant. I was the younger child in a small family. Every morning I retched for a half-hour after waking, and for weeks I thought I had some terrible disease—one far worse than, but related to, the nausea that had afflicted me the year before. I had never been around anyone who was pregnant, and I had never heard of morning sickness. Dan, the eldest child in his large family, knew exactly what was wrong, but I couldn't—wouldn't—hear him telling me so. "I'm *sick*," I kept telling him. "Really, really *sick*." Despite my insistence, however, I found myself careful not to mention my illness to my mother. I was determined not to worry her. She was working, she had Sally to worry about, she was still trying to settle Daddy's estate. She had enough on her mind.

One warm morning in early June, I woke up feeling surprisingly well. I sat up, then gingerly stood up on the fluffy white throw rug beside my bed. No nausea! My mother and sister were still sleeping, though it was nearly six-thirty, and I knew their alarm clocks would go off soon. I went to the bathroom and then wandered out to the kitchen. On the counter was a brown wooden bowl filled with warm, fresh cherries. Delicious. I picked it up, opened the side door, and stepped out onto the patio. It was going to be a hot day—it was hot already. I sat at the picnic table eating cherries, trying to decide what to wear to school that morning. School was almost out for the summer, and I was glad. It had been a hard year, and I was not doing well.

Soon I heard doors inside begin to open and shut. I got up, absent-mindedly leaving the bowl of cherries on the picnic table, and went to my room to dress. As soon as I closed my bedroom door behind me, I threw up. The undigested cherries splattered onto the white rug. Sweating, I reached down to fold up the rug, when another wave of nausea emptied the rest of the glistening, red mass onto the floor.

I crouched and listened. The door to the hall bathroom opened. My mother's bedroom door was still closed. The trick would be to get the mess from my room to the bathroom without intersecting my mother's path from her room to the kitchen. I cracked my door, looked and listened, dashed for the bathroom, and locked the door behind me.

I spent a long time in the shower that morning, ignoring my mother's pleas about the hot water as I scrubbed the little rug and watched the red muck swirl down the bathtub drain. I had been praying for a different red stain, the longed-for sign that could save me, but this did not come.

When my breasts began to swell and ache, I told Dan I was afraid

I had cancer. *"You are pregnant!"* he shouted. "That is one of the signs!" Together we went to the telephone book, picked out the name of a gynecologist whose office was at some distance from our neighborhood, and made an appointment.

The following week, after school, I drove to the doctor's office in a small shopping center. I used a made-up name, Margaret Morgan, I think—something unfortunately close to my own—on the forms I was asked to fill out. When the nurse called the fake name, I went in, sat across a desk from the gentleman in the white coat, and explained my situation, including the fact that my father had just died and I didn't think my mother could cope if I turned out to be pregnant. The doctor wrote a prescription for three pills. After I was done with them, my period would come—unless I was pregnant.

I took the prescription for Margaret Morgan, but I didn't get up from the chair. I had read a *Saturday Evening Post* series about something called abortion. The articles had described illegal abortions, coathanger deaths, gangrene wards, desperate women, desperate girls. I had some sense that abortions were illegal everywhere, but I wasn't sure, so I asked the doctor if he knew how I could get a safe one.

The doctor jumped up from his desk, threw open the door to his office, and told me loudly to get out. Women in maternity smocks and others with new babies in their arms and toddlers playing at their feet watched as a slender, pony-tailed fifteen-year-old in a flowered shirtwaist dress ran through the reception area, gripping her purse in one hand and a prescription in the other.

Dan and I knew nothing would come of the pills, but I couldn't help being guardedly hopeful.

Another week ticked by. There was no longer any way I could deny what was happening to me.

Thirty years later, I thought about that callous doctor and the climate of opinion that allowed—perhaps even forced—a medical professional to behave so cruelly.

I recently found an article from the mid-1960s, widely cited by researchers for many years, by a doctor named James P. Cattell, titled "Psychodynamic and Clinical Observations in a Group of Unmarried Mothers." It appears in *The Unwed Mother,* a collection of twenty-one articles by seventeen men and four women published in 1966 (the year after my son was born). Based on "54 consecutive referrals" who "were seen once or twice in psychiatric consultation," Cattell reported that "the following distribution of diagnoses was found: character disorder, 30; neurotic reaction, 7 (anxiety, depressive, and onversion); schizophrenia, 17 (pseudoneurotic, 7; other types, 10)."

Not one sane woman in the bunch! I don't know where I, at sixteen, would have fit in Dr. Cattell's group, but although I believe my own emotional health was seriously impaired at the time of my pregnancy and beyond, it is difficult for me to imagine how this researcher found a third of his subjects to be suffering from schizophrenia, even allowing for the common diagnostic errors of those years, when many people were hung with that stigmatizing label.

Also in *The Unwed Mother* was an article by a social worker named Rose Bernstein titled "Are We Still Stereotyping the Unmarried Mother?" Bernstein clearly believed that indeed "we" were. She argued that "Personality traits registered at a time of crisis . . . can be interpreted in only a limited way as ongoing characteristics of the unmarried mother, individually or as a group."

Bernstein was fighting an uphill battle: I found fewer references to her article in subsequent research. In the same collection, however, was an article called "Personality Patterns in Unmarried Mothers," by Leontine R. Young, that, like Cattell's study, seemed to have been picked up by researchers for years afterward. Young surmised that the pregnancies of unmarried women had been deliberately, if unconsciously, conceived. "It is not coincidence that one almost never finds a girl, however intelligent or educated, who has thought of contraceptives or has ever considered the possibility of an abortion as a solution to her problem," wrote Young.

It was lucky for the purity of Young's findings that she had never met one like me.

Young had her reasons for an unwed mother's behavior, which, though my reason comprehended them not, I had to admit were juicy: "What better revenge could she devise against a rejecting mother than to bear an illegitimate child and place the responsibility for him upon her mother's shoulders?" That argument could have been used to describe my situation, I thought.

It was easy to slip into the molds Young constructed. I would have found her more persuasive, however, if I had not just read a heartbreaking memoir, *The House of Tomorrow,* by Jean Thompson (a pseudonym), who upon finding herself pregnant in college in the early sixties had set up an elaborate system of evasions to keep her well-bred, academic parents from learning her secret. Alone, she moved to a strange city, found a Salvation Army home, earned her keep by working as an au pair with a prying local couple, gave birth to her child, and, alone, gave him up to a family she had chosen carefully, in a private, legal adoption. All without placing one iota of responsibility on her mother's—or anyone else's—shoulders.

Young punctuated her article with protestations of neutrality: "The writer is well aware that to generalize about unmarried mothers, as about any group of human beings, may be both rash and misleading." "To discuss common trends in the personality patterns of 100 girls can be a snare and a delusion." Yet it seemed she couldn't help herself. "All these girls," she concluded a few paragraphs later, "had fundamental problems in their relationships with other people."

Tell us about it! Take their boyfriends, for instance, who in many cases abandoned the women they had impregnated. It would be two decades before sociologist Edwin M. Schur perceptively noted in his book *Labeling Women Deviant* that "there really is no widespread deviance labeling of 'unwed fathers.' "

As a society, we are no longer shocked by an "unwed mother," especially one who is older and self-supporting, whether or not we approve of her. And researchers no longer spend so much time and ink on articles about the hidden hostilities of the pregnant teenager.

In her 1992 book *Wake Up Little Susie: Single Pregnancy and Race*

Before Roe v. Wade, historian Rickie Solinger wrote about those of us in my generation who became pregnant accidentally: "While these girls were viewed as rebels or misfits because they had had nonmarital sex and gotten pregnant, it is much more likely that they were part of a horde of unfortunate girl-pioneers who became sexually active in the historical moment just before such behavior was widely recognized as typical and just before they had a chance to protect themselves from the consequences."

Whether or not Dan and I could have "protected ourselves from the consequences," and whether or not I was emotionally disturbed, the fact that we were young and fertile had something to do with what happened to us. In trying to fight stereotyping, Rose Bernstein suggested that the single trait all unmarried mothers had in common was their fertility, which in some appeared to be exceptional. I became pregnant during my first act of sexual intercourse. To discern pathology in that seemed to me as useless, insensitive, and inappropriate as asking a woman hoping to adopt a child why she didn't just have her own.

One night when I came home from a date with Dan, my mother was sitting on my bed, gripping the empty prescription bottle that had held the confirming three pills. Her face was set in rigid challenge. She had found the bottle as, in accordance with good psychiatric theory, I suppose I must have intended her to do, and had looked up the doctor in the phone book. Finding that he was a gynecologist, she realized I must have gone to him secretly.

"What the hell is this all about?" she demanded.

On the spot, I smoothly invented a lie, telling her the pills belonged to a classmate whose last name was, indeed, Morgan, who had given me the bottle . . . for some reason. What could I have said that made my mother drop her interrogation and leave the room? What could possibly convince her that I was telling the truth? She had already noticed that there were no tampons in the trash each month. Now she'd found a pill bottle from a gynecologist. She nonetheless managed to avoid putting two-and-two together. My easy lies simply buttressed her remarkable ability to avoid what she did not want to know.

For me, it was different. I could think of nothing else. I sat in my classes at school unable to respond if a teacher called my name. My friend Debbie, a very upright, serious-minded, ethical girl, would tilt her test papers my way in French class, obviously to make them easier for me to copy. Somehow, in spite of the rectitude with which she conducted her life, she sensed my despair and knew I needed help. She was right. I could think only one thought, over and over again: What am I going to do now? What am I going to do now?

Dan wanted to marry me. My interpretation of his loyalty, arrived at with admittedly scant evidence and at great distance, is that he was even more dependent on me than I was on him. He never seemed anxious or worried about my pregnancy. On the contrary, he seemed positively happy about it, even peaceful. But whatever the reason, he did stick by me, and in that way my story is different from those of many girls and women, then and now, who have been unsupported by their partners.

We spent our time mimicking ordinary high-school students, but we began to make vague plans. We would marry: that was our plan, but it simply did not happen, and now I have forgotten why. We had a habit, on our weekend dates, of going to a certain restaurant for shrimp cocktails and coffee. We would sit across a small table from each other and of course we would talk; once the fact of my pregnancy became indisputable it was difficult to talk about anything else. But what we said eludes me now. Not one word comes back.

Toward the end of the school year, there were also other, more immediate, less challenging plans to make. Dan was a graduating senior; I had to shop for a prom dress. At Lord & Taylor, I found the perfect one. I could probably sew a copy of that dress from memory, it was so pretty and I remember it so well—light blue satin with a beaded bodice and narrow straplike shoulders, and a full skirt that fell to my toes. It was nearly identical to the dress Walt Disney's Cinderella wore to the fateful ball, minus only the organza puff sleeves and peplum.

The day of the prom, I went to a beauty shop to have my hair done, in a simple, elegant coif that also looked a lot like the fairygodmother's handiwork. Bibbity, bobbity, boo: A lovely young girl going to a fancy dress ball. Two months along.

Dan was accepted at two colleges, one in Maryland and one in the Midwest, where his family had come from originally. He hadn't chosen either. Instead, in late June, he joined the navy. Not, he explained, to leave me: It would be a month or more before he had to leave for basic training. No. He wanted us to marry. But he had enlisted in a special program of only six months' active service, with an obligation of subsequent reserve duty, he said, because his father, a high-ranking navy officer, had urged him to make himself safe from the draft. It was 1964. Dan's father undoubtedly knew that what was then usually called the "skirmish" in Vietnam would soon heat up. Dan's father had only his son's best interests at heart, and Dan, as he himself insisted, had only ours. He repeatedly assured me that this way he would never again have to leave us, his wife and child. Within a couple of years I would know that he could have gotten a college deferment, or a family deferment. It was also perfectly possible he would never have been drafted. I now suspect that Dan felt secure pursuing whatever path he wanted because in his mind the pregnancy sealed our fate: We would be together forever. Or something like that.

The clock began to strike midnight during the summer. My breasts became so tender I couldn't sleep on my stomach. At first I was so thin I could feel my swollen womb like a large, firm egg in my abdomen. Then I began to bloat a bit in the middle. I went almost daily to the community pool to which we belonged, and I wore a two-piece suit from the year before. "It's still perfectly good," my mother said, when I asked if we couldn't go shopping for another. I wanted a one-piece, but she was clear: "We don't have the money." I sat on a towel a lot that year, wearing a terrycloth coverup and playing solitaire.

Luckily, baby-doll dresses came into fashion. At fifteen, I was just the right age for the gathered, figure-hiding smocks. I remember one I had in pink gingham, quite childish, like something a two-year-old might wear.

That summer I signed up for a special science seminar, because biology was the only subject I'd done well in the year before. It was not just the subject that I liked, but my teacher, Mr. Baker, a quiet, gentle man who was the only adult at my school who acknowledged my father's death. He had been waiting for me after Christmas vacation. Whisking me into the hall, where we could have some privacy in the crowd, he took my hand and held it for a moment. "I am so sorry about your father," he said, looking at me closely and trying, I think, to see if I was all right. I was so numb then that I didn't answer, but I was not so numb that I didn't care.

Mr. Baker ran the summer seminar, for which we visited such fascinating places as an experimental animal farm in Beltsville, Maryland, where a calf ate part of my skirt, and a naval testing center, where the hydrodynamics and flotation of ship models were analyzed in a room-size tank of water in which different types of currents and storms could be simulated. Everywhere we went it was hot—it was summer, this was Washington—and everywhere we went we stood still to listen to the lecturers who showed us around. The first time I fainted, someone caught me before I hit the floor. The next few times, I was able to recognize the warning signs—the cold sweat, my tongue sticking to the roof of my mouth—and I either leaned over or sat down in time to prevent a fall. I often wore the pink gingham dress, which looked much like a maternity dress, and I am sure Mr. Baker twigged to my condition. He remained extraordinarily kind to me.

To my shellshocked mother I suppose all appeared normal. Normal had not been normal at our house in years, so it was difficult to assess the family condition. To me, life was surreal, going on around me in an astonishingly robust way while I was secretly ill, secretly heartsick, secretly panic-stricken.

Dan and I still went to the same now-forgotten woods. One

moonlit night, he reached over to remove the strap of what he thought was my bra, to find it was only the white line left by my bathing-suit top. "Try to take *that* off," I said. I began to chuckle, then to laugh, and then I couldn't stop. Dan sat quietly for a while, observing my hysteria. Then he began to laugh with me—what else could he do? We laughed and laughed until I thought I would throw up; I was sick with laughter.

I had to stop going to church, though I had spent a lot of my childhood and teenage years in Sunday School or Methodist Youth Fellowship or the choir. Now that I was pregnant, standing to sing was guaranteed to make me drop. It was embarrassing to sit down in the middle of a hymn, in front of the congregation. And besides, I was by now beginning to lose even that minimal faith that had made church services possible for me.

Sometime in July, I think, when I was over three months along, Dan and I finally realized that our time was up.

First, we told my mother. Sitting on the brown couch in our living room, I said simply, "Dan and I are going to get married."

"You're going to what?" she said, with either sarcasm or disbelief.

"Get married," I repeated. "And," I added, "we're going to have a baby."

My mother's reaction was instantaneous and explosive. "How could you DO this to me?" she shrieked.

I didn't know how to answer. I had known she would take it hard, and I truly hated causing her pain, but when I considered her question literally, I knew that I had never intended to do anything at all to her, certainly not something like this. I had not thought of her once, in fact, while achieving this remarkable feat of negligence and irresponsibility.

"I didn't do it to *you,* Mama," I answered, trying to find a way to tell her how much I regretted it all, but she kept screaming, "How? HOW? How *could* you?"

Many occasions and events in the preceding years had left me speechless, and this was yet another. I stopped trying to talk and just looked at my fingers in my lap until my mother stopped screaming.

Finally, she quieted down. Her gaze emptied. "I never thought anything bad could happen to you while you were wearing Daddy's ring," she said dazedly. She shook her head. "How far along are you?"

"Since April."

"Jesus Christ. It's too late for an abortion. Why the *hell* didn't you tell me before now?"

My head shot up and I could feel my pulse pounding in my temples. I instinctively put my hand over my heart, as if to slow it down. Was it possible? Did ordinary women like my mother know how to get abortions? It was dizzying to me to think that confiding in her might have ended my ordeal. Confiding in my mother was something I had stopped doing many years earlier.

The following days were filled with humiliation, as my mother and then Dan's father alternately derided and harangued us.

Dan's father was domineering, but his mother was a kind, pretty, soft-spoken woman. Alone of our three parents, she never directed a single wounding remark my way. I was in the sort of emotional state where even a hard look made me bow my head in shame. She not only never looked at me that way, but when her husband asked us such contemptuous questions as "What makes you think you could raise a child?" it was she, my silent, helpless ally, whose eyes turned down. (Was there really someone in the world who cared for me, in my predicament? Cared even more for me, because of it?)

I imagine that Dan expected me to be like his mother—deferential, peaceable, amenable. I felt none of those things. I felt desperate—sleeplessly, unremittingly desperate. But it's possible that in my utter dependency, and especially in my stunned near-silence, I may have appeared docile.

Dan and I neglected to marry before he left for boot camp. I wish I could remember exactly how that occurred, or, I mean, *didn't* occur. I can only surmise that because we needed my mother's signature we could not do it without her help, and that helping us to marry was the farthest thing from her mind.

There was nothing about us any more that was a twosome. We were now a problem surrounded by parents. I can't recall being alone with Dan again. I don't know how he left, when he left, or what we said. The only thing I know with certainty is that despite my desperation, I was unable to persuade Dan to stay.

"Please," I said, my eyes unblinking. If I'd had tears, I would have been prepared to shed them then. But I didn't, and hadn't since my father's death. It was a strange dry spell for a Moorman.

"Please stay here, with me."

Dan seemed to be on a trajectory. He had a look of certainty and a slight but chilling air of benign condescension as he held my shoulders in his hands and explained why this would be the best thing for both of us—for all of us. For some reason this particular scene occurred out of doors, in the late afternoon, on the rocky, unevenly paved front walk of my house. I remember tilting backward slightly on a loose stone, watching the sun streak through the branches of a locust tree in the middle distance, behind his left shoulder. I remember the way he smoothed his long brown hair away from his high forehead.

I may remember that moment so clearly because it was the precise point at which any love I might have felt toward this boy was forever blocked.

If I had been anxious and frightened before, I now perfected the shell of numbness that had already begun to cover the soft, unprotected core of my being. For the next twenty years, in any time of stress, that barrier provided my one great stay against despair.

2

Unwed mothers at that time ... were a specific group; they fell somewhere between criminals and patients and, like criminals and patients, they were prescribed an exact and fortifying treatment: They were made to disappear.

Alice McDermott, *That Night*

DAN LEFT FOR BASIC TRAINING. Now there was no one left in Arlington who believed that he and I would marry.

"You don't need to compound your mistake," my mother kept saying, and I came to believe she was right about that. With hindsight, I can glimpse a half-dozen other times, later than this one, when she said something similarly subversive to me about one man or another. "You don't have to stay with him," she remarked with an understated shrug, as if that offhand gesture could mask the dramatic nature of her proposition. Of course in a way she was right—I didn't have to stay with anyone. I could be alone, be at home, be with her, cook her meals, keep her company.

Whatever my mother's motives may have been, the truth was that I was too young to establish a family of my own. I was too young for the responsibility of independence from my own family. I had just turned sixteen; I had only recently stopped growing. But even more than my youth, my profound sorrow made me unfit for motherhood. How could I put another's needs before my own?

I have thought about it a lot. When I read Maya Angelou's collection of essays, *Wouldn't Take Nothing For My Journey Now,* and came to the sentence "I was a twenty-one-year-old single parent with my son in kindergarten," I stopped short and wondered if maybe I, too, couldn't have made a go of it. So many times I have revisited this question. I sometimes imagine that a baby might have distracted me and provided me with determination, through love. I know plenty of unexpected children who have done that for their surprised, sudden parents. But none of their mothers was quite so disturbed as I was. In one of Dan's letters he expressed his wrenching dismay at my admission that I didn't know if I could go on. The love I really needed was not that of a child, whose ability to provide love should be the last emotional resource of the parent. The love I needed was my mother's. I had not had her positive attention since my sister returned from the hospital. My mother and I had been very close when I was a child, but whether it was my adolescence or my sister's demanding illness or my father's death that robbed me of her love, it had seemed to diminish until I had no real relationship with her at all.

I could easily guess what my mother wanted me to do now, and I was incapable of resisting, especially after Dan left. She was the one I desperately needed, and it was increasingly clear that she would be the only one there for me, even if her presence was hardly comforting, even if it was completely without visible affection.

In the mid-1960s, teen pregnancy was on a steep rise, and adoption, at least for girls who were white and middle-class, had become almost routine. Our parents must have known this, even if we didn't. When I told Dan's father and mother that I was going to give the baby up for adoption, we were sitting in their living room. I sat alone facing the front windows of the house, looking out at the street I'd grown up on. Dan's father and mother sat across from me in separate armchairs.

"I've decided to give the baby up for adoption," I said flatly, looking from one to the other, expecting nothing, but catching a look of self-satisfaction on his father's face that made me stiffen. In an instant, I knew that I was playing a role I'd been groomed for from the moment Dan and I had told them I was pregnant. I had at last made the right move, and they had cunningly engineered it in such a way that it was my own decision—nothing they could be blamed for. Unfortunately, my momentary horror at the discovery that I might be only their puppet was blurred by the fact that I no longer wanted to marry Dan anyway. I was beginning to hate him for having left me there to deal with our parents alone, to deal with my life alone, to deal with the pregnancy alone, and my budding resentment made it all a little easier.

These days it is considered politically incorrect in some circles to use the phrase "give the baby up." One "places the baby for adoption" now, or "makes an adoption plan." It is a comforting stylistic change, a euphemism that puts a positive slant on the mother's decision and emphasizes her active role. Although some birth mothers do "place" their babies, in that they may choose from among many available would-be parents, their decision to make that kind of choice is still prompted by the same desperation that led me to give up my child. Shame, the likelihood of poverty, the lack of familial support: these are the elements of the atmosphere surrounding the girl or woman who gives up her child. It isn't as if in "placing" her child she is simply moving to the next step in a plan that she deliberately set in motion by becoming pregnant in the first place.

An adoptive parent has told me that the new phraseology is a way of protecting children from the stigma of being an "unwanted" child. I can see how it might do that in some cases, for some children. But I think there is a kernel of truth in any adoption—that the child was relinquished by the woman in whose womb she grew—that can't, in the end, be disguised by happier words. To me, that is a sad fact, even if the woman chose the adoptive parents for her baby and gave her gift wholeheartedly and with a sense of peace. No matter how proactive the birth mother's decision may seem, it is always a response to what seems at the time an impossible situation.

My friend Margaret, a psychotherapist, says, "Oh, I see adoptees all the time. They all want to know, 'Why was I given up?' " I asked Margaret if she thought that the words "given up" were, in themselves, stigmatizing. I asked her if she thought it would have made a difference to her clients if they had been told their birth mothers had made an adoption plan.

"I don't know," Margaret said. "I think that for adoptees who have problems related to their adoption, given up is given up." A loss by any other name is still a loss.

The critical distinction to be made, it seems to me, is the one between an unwanted pregnancy and the child who results from it. An unwanted pregnancy does not necessarily result in an unwanted child. Pregnancy has a firm deadline, and all decisions about what will happen at the deadline are made by a woman whose hormones are in flux and whose life is in crisis. Even married women who carry unwanted pregnancies to term have been known to thank God, over the years, for the blessing that resulted. I have a friend who, as a tired young mother of four, was so sure she could not go through with her fifth pregnancy she consulted an old woman who, she'd heard, had a potion that would bring on a miscarriage. That night, trying to warm herself near the fireplace and holding the vial of medicine the woman had given her, my friend stared into flames and tried to summon the courage to go through with her plan. Her husband and children were asleep upstairs. Finally, she opened the bottle and held it up, but before she could drink the liquid she found herself tossing it into the fire instead, where it made a bright blue flame shoot up with a hiss. She went to bed, telling herself she would just have to find a way to cope, somehow. The fifth child, like each of her siblings, was—still is—a joy. It seems plausible to me that one could feel unable to cope and yet find a way to do it once the crisis becomes a baby. A baby is more loveable than a pregnancy, especially an accidental pregnancy.

In Rael Jean Isaac's book *Adopting a Child Today,* published in 1965, the year I delivered, I learned that I had been merely part of a trend, which can be a comforting thought to the guilt-stricken. "While there has been a 100 per cent increase in the rate of out-of-wedlock births for girls under twenty in the last twenty years, which is substantial enough, there has been a 400 per cent increase for girls between twenty and twenty-four, and a 500 per cent increase for women between twenty-five and twenty-nine in the same period."

Isaac reported that seventy per cent of white unwed mothers gave up their children for adoption.

I have always seen my situation as being defined by, above all, the fact that I had no alternative, but Isaac saw adoption in a completely different light. "The mother's limited resources are not the chief reason that so many babies are relinquished for adoption," she wrote. "Although the popular explanation is that the mother gives up her child in order to give it the opportunity to have the normal family life she cannot provide—and to give herself the chance to resume the normal course of her life which the baby had interrupted—fundamentally the unmarried mother relinquishes her child because society expects her to do so. . . . The mother accepts adoption as the best solution for providing for her baby's future because she has been told it is the best solution.

The clearest demonstration of this is in the relative proportion of mothers who give up their children in the U.S. and in some of the European countries. If the comparison is confined to white unmarried mothers, . . . in England only 20 per cent and in Denmark only 7 per cent do so. In Denmark the state provides apartment blocks where all women without husbands may take apartments, whether they are widowed, divorced, or unmarried mothers. . . . The community thus makes it comparatively easy for the mother to keep her child, and 93 per cent of mothers do so despite the large number of Danish couples eager to adopt.

My first choice would have been to have an abortion, right away. I wanted to live as normal a life as I could—I *still* want that—and at sixteen that meant being a high-school junior. But although I admit that in giving up my son I made my own choice, the years have taught me what I could never have suspected at the time: that I was poorly prepared for that choice. I don't know if I would have made it if I had known that the aftermath of such a decision could be so devastating.

I am sure it never occurred to me or my mother that I could just keep the baby, as a woman I met as an adult did during the same years, the mid-1960s. The latter woman's family helped her rear her daughter until she herself had finished college and was mature enough to take care of the little girl on her own. What were the spoken words that enabled that to happen, that enabled them to shape an agreement by which a young daughter was able to keep her baby, and by which her parents were able to keep their first grandchild? When I met this woman and her daughter, the mother was in her mid-thirties, an artist married to another artist, and her daughter was entering college. They looked like sisters, but the relationship was clearly one of parent and child, judging from the nature of their conversation. And yet this mother had been only seventeen when she gave birth. I tentatively told her of my experience. "Oh," she said, "My parents were *fierce* about keeping the baby."

Fierce! My mother was fierce, too, but not about keeping her grandchild. I am not able to conjure up an image of either of my parents fiercely keeping an illegitimate child. My mother and father had already hidden Sally's illness—she had been "away at school" (without a break or a vacation) for a year and a half. A baby is harder to hide. And yet this baby could so easily, with their help, have been made legitimate.

I wanted to call Dan long distance—still something of a luxury in those days—to tell him of my decision, but his father wouldn't hear of it. "You can tell him in person," he said. "He can hear it from the horse's mouth."

In a blithe breach of military rules easily arranged by the captain, I was allowed to visit Dan in Alabama. I had been on a train once, to Baltimore, but I had never traveled by air. Dan's father and I flew on a small propeller plane, leaving from National Airport one gray morning. There were storms all the way south, and the plane's wings shook. On the left one, outside my window, I could see an enormous patch, a yard in diameter, of what looked like strips of masking tape, as if a huge hole in the metal had been fixed up quickly by someone using school supplies. It didn't look right; it looked unsafe; and as we rattled through the clouds I acquired an uncharacteristic serenity. Nothing mattered now. I was confident that we would all die before we reached our destination.

An hour later, Dan's father and I were in a rented car, on our way to the base. I had changed in a ladies' room at the airport. It was unbearably, wetly hot, so I put on my best white heels without stockings. I wore a slim, turquoise-blue, linen two-piece dress that I had made myself, and white gloves. My hair was in a heavily-sprayed flip, but it began to frizz with the humidity.

As Dan's father and I were entering the military compound, he turned and looked me up and down. "I used to see you after church and think, what a nice girl." He shook his head and looked away.

Dan's head was shaved, I could tell, even though he was in full uniform, hat and all. I hadn't realized how much his tan forelock had contributed to his overall looks, but now his face, without its frame, frightened me. I hoped he would keep his hat on, so I wouldn't have to see the full effect.

He was thrilled to have me there and still seemed somehow surprised, although he'd known we were coming. I didn't tell him why right away. He shook hands with his father, who then went to pace in the distance, a damp mirage in my peripheral vision, but one that exerted a powerful force. He was anxious that I get it over with. He was afraid I might change my mind, or that Dan would change it for me. He had nothing to worry about.

Dan talked excitedly about how well he was doing in boot camp. He had passed various tests with flying colors and been offered a position in officers' training school after boot camp; he could do x number of pushups in x minutes. I looked at Dan, a middle-class boy, and wondered why this was so thrilling to him.

I realize now that I didn't know much about Dan. I don't think he had distinguished himself in high school particularly. His excellence in boot camp—both because he was physically strong and because he was smart—gave him self-confidence that he had not had before. In particular, it enabled him to hold up his head in front of his macho father.

I, on the other hand, was bored and thoroughly alienated. Dan pointed to some troops marching in formation and described how they had to drill in the sun. Sometimes a flag was hoisted that signalled unsafe temperatures, but usually a few troops had fainted from the heat by then. Dan laughed heartily.

This is sick, I thought, with unaccustomed clarity. Dan took off his hat and pressed his sleeve to his sweaty forehead. I looked away from the stubble on his skull and saw his father striding energetically, with choreographed aimlessness, keeping to the shade of a low building in a distant corner of the base.

"I'm going to give the baby up for adoption," I said quickly, unaccountably flinching, as if Dan might swing at me.

Dan gave me his attention. I could see a number of looks pass over his face: disbelief, anger, pain, resolve. He may have tried to talk me out of my decision, but I don't remember his words. At one point he looked as if he might cry. Again, I looked away, but in a concession to what I saw as decency and continuity, I think I told him I would marry him after high school, and that we could raise a family then.

"But what are you going to do?" Dan asked.

"I told you—give up the baby for adoption."

"But how?"

Until now, the phrase "give the baby up for adoption" had been enough. It had satisfied the parents, resolved my dilemma, and given me a goal. However, I could now see that, as a plan, it lacked detail.

Later that evening, Dan's father took me to dinner before we flew back to Washington. Once upon a time, when I was still just a young girl who lived in the neighborhood, I had troubled to be outgoing to this man, as I was to all my friends' parents. Now, though, I had nothing to offer him, not even my attention, however distracted. So now it was he who tried to charm me, smiling and telling stories, trying to elicit some interest. As I stared at the remains of my meal, I gradually became aware that he seemed to be trying to make our dinner into a kind of date, one during which the couple converses politely, nodding and smiling and making small talk.

Ever amenable, as a southern girl, to playing the hostess, but knowing I needed fortification that evening, I ordered a cup of coffee. The captain ordered one too. When they came, I noticed that the waitress had placed the cream pitcher on his side of the table. I waited a decent moment in case he planned to use it and then, after he took a sip of coffee, asked if he would please pass it to me.

He looked at me. I waited. My face became hot. Finally he pushed the pitcher in my direction and looked away, shaking his head slightly. "If you have to put cream in it," he said, "you don't really like coffee."

My mother made an appointment at the Florence Crittenden Home and Hospital for unwed mothers in Washington. She also telephoned a respected adoption agency called the Winnicott Foundation. She seemed to know all about this business. I had never heard anyone discuss either out-of-wedlock pregnancy (which was what I was experiencing now that I was not on my way to becoming a bride), maternity homes, or adoption agencies, but apparently there was a whole world beyond sour French teachers and proms, one that was known to adults, even to my mother. I went along. I went along. I got up each morning, and went along.

The day we visited the Crittenden home was hot and heavily overcast. We drove with all the car windows down but perspiring nonetheless. Mother's face had been set in a grim, unfocused stare from the moment she woke up. She kept her eyes on the road as we drove over Key Bridge and swung onto the Whitehurst Freeway.

In a 1965 book on adoption, the home was listed in the appendix of resources for pregnant girls and women: "District of Columbia, Florence Crittenden Home and Hospital. Service is regardless of age or religion, but Negro girls are referred to other sources. Fee is scaled according to ability to pay."

The home may have seemed more foreboding than it would have on a day that had some starch in it. But immediately on entering its dim and silent corridors (were the girls and women told to stay in their rooms?), I refused to complete the interview and tour. I simply balked, with a will that could not be cracked. My mother tried to argue, but not with any conviction.

My mother tended to identify with me to a perhaps unhealthy extent. When someone paid me a compliment her response ("Why, aren't *you* sweet!") would be out of her mouth before I had a chance to open mine. But at the Crittenden Home my mother's fuzzy boundaries worked to my advantage. The two of us shared a need for bountiful light, and I am sure she found the place as depressing as I did. She could not bring herself to consign me, or the part of me that would always feel like—and be like—her, to this above-ground dungeon.

Driving home from the Crittenden visit, Mama paid me a compliment, one that startled me both by its simplicity and by its uniqueness in those months of bitter disappointment. I immediately stored it away in a tiny, interior, velvet-lined box, separate from the many other looks, words, and actions of that miserable time. "You were smart to put your hair up in a pony tail," she said, pushing down on the turn signal and swerving into the lefthand lane. Her own hair was short and curly. She reached behind her head and smoothed it up temporarily. "I wish I could get mine off my neck. I'm hot as hell."

I was relieved. She seemed relaxed too. It was a mystery to me then, but now I can guess what subconscious feelings were at work that day. From time to time for the rest of her life, Mother would say she missed having Daddy around to make decisions—she hated being alone and even worse hated taking sole responsibility for important moves. On this particularly depressing day, I had helped her make a decision simply by taking a stand and refusing to budge. The place was a prison, or so we thought. Prison was unfitting punishment for a crime of passion.

That doesn't entirely explain it. When I was in the Crittenden home, I suddenly understood what should have been the most obvious fact about the place: that those who entered its doors were other pregnant girls and women. I don't know if I thought of them as bad girls—or "cheap" girls, as we put it then—as opposed to unlucky me, or if I thought of them as unintelligent girls, as opposed to college-bound me, or if I just thought of them as a group whose visible presence would make it impossible for me to maintain my chrysalis of denial, which had become my main source of hope. I didn't want to face my situation. I was ashamed. I couldn't imagine meeting others who would know exactly how I'd come to be where I was. I couldn't bear the thought of becoming one of a number of young women like me. I wasn't ready to abandon the fantasy that this problem of mine was somehow an illusion.

There was also an aspect of my childhood that made sisterhood suspect to me, and always would, to some degree. While I may have felt a hundred years old in my heart, I would have been, in fact, some years younger than the average Crittenden resident. Many were in their twenties, or older. To some young girls, the age difference, with its implicit suggestion of guidance and protection, would have been a solace, but I had an older sister who was at that time nothing but a source of embarrassment and anxiety to me. For me, it was essential to be different from Sally in order to convince myself that I wouldn't become like her—so downcast, so solitary, so full of rage. I couldn't afford to become like the other girls at Crittenden. I might turn out like Sally: I might never recover.

My mother, for her part, had already institutionalized her first problem child. Sally had gone to the hospital a docile, if catatonically depressed, youth, and she had emerged an angry young woman with ideas about just how much she could take of her mother's frequently expressed disapproval and disappointment. Sally's fury rocked the rafters, and it made the house unbearable for me, but as the other child of that disappointed mother I later understood the necessity for Sally's defensive rage. I have a feeling our mother may semiconsciously have looked at Crittenden as another place in which a daughter could be taken away from her and offered perspective, and with it independence.

Recently, I was put in touch by telephone with someone who had gone into "Flo Crit" as a pregnant teenager in the early sixties.

"Was it dark?" I asked.

"Was what dark?"

"It seemed like a dungeon the day I visited."

"Oh, that was the old front building, probably," she said. "There was a new dorm in back, where we lived. It was wonderful. I was the youngest in the place—you probably would have been, too—and the older girls really took me under their wing. Oh, it was great to be out of your family's house. Away from those *looks*. Remember the looks?"

I remembered the looks. As I listened to her talk, I rued my long-ago decision. Instead of going into "Flo Crit," where reality would have been unavoidable, I had clung to the appearance of normalness. Many people were clinging to that where I grew up, when I grew up—in the South, in the fifties and early sixties, in the suburbs. We didn't know it, I suppose. Everyone looked all right. I wonder, did we all look fine to the people who actually *were* fine? Or were the parents of those truly all right families murmuring over their morning coffee about this alcoholic bureaucrat, or that wild son of the minister's, or the girl across the road who was sneaking out of her bedroom window late each night, minding the shrubs as she tiptoed off to meet her boyfriend waiting on the corner?

The truth was, I was sixteen and pregnant and not locked to wed the father of the child (What child? Was this problem I had actually going to be a child?), and I was frightened for my sanity. I was much less protected against the possible disintegration of my psyche than even my sister, who had at least received some intensive treatment and who had faced her most private demons and was no longer afraid of them. For me the truth was out of the question. If I was going to go on living (an *if* that I considered seriously and with some frequency) I was going to do it with the blessed help of denial. In denial, I could maintain my optimistic notion that not only was this not happening (easier now that my mother shared so much of the panic that for months had been mine alone), but also that this would all be over soon. My life would once again merrily roll along, the way it had before.

Hadn't it?

In yet another moment of resourcefulness, my mother remembered a friend of a friend who rented rooms to young women from colleges in southern Virginia who came up to Arlington to student-teach in the county's highly-rated school system. My mother called this person, explained our situation, mentioned that no one, including their mutual acquaintance, knew about our trouble, and asked if she would consider taking me in as a boarder for the remaining months of my pregnancy.

It was almost the end of the summer. I was not showing, exactly, but I could no longer wear most of my shirtwaist dresses. The baby-doll dresses seemed eerily hyper-appropriate, considering the secret I was supposedly keeping, so I stopped wearing them. Clothes were a problem. In those days, invitations to parties or receptions usually included an important five-letter word: "heels" or "flats." That told us exactly what to wear. Heels signified the sort of clothes I wore when I went to tell Dan I was giving the baby up for adoption—a linen suit or a good (Sunday) dress. Flats meant a shirtwaist dress or a blouse and skirt. With heels one usually wore stockings and often wore or carried white gloves. With flats, stockings were optional, and gloves were out.

To meet Mrs. Blake, the woman with rooms to rent, I wore flats. I wouldn't have worn heels anyway, but I no longer had the choice. None of my good clothes fit. The only decent dress that would fasten around my slim but thickening middle was a Villager shirtwaist with a fresh and innocent pattern of blue cornflowers. It was the one I had worn to consult the obstetrician who threw me out of his office when I asked about abortion. It had some elastic in the waist and a stretch jute belt with blue leather ends, and I wore it whenever I wanted to look nice. I had to look nice for Mrs. Blake.

"We'll be lucky if she says yes," Mother said doubtfully. She thought for a minute. "It's almost September. If she takes you in, it'll look like you went away to school." Sure, I thought. Why not? We'd already used that story, when Sally was in the mental hospital. Maybe it had worked then; maybe it would work now.

The next evening, we drove to Mrs. Blake's house, inconveniently but significantly located far from our neighborhood. Mrs.

Blake, a pretty, round-cheeked woman with bright blue eyes, answered the door wearing an expression of absolute neutrality. Very formally, she invited us in.

Sitting behind her in an armchair in the living room was her mother, an elderly Dutch woman introduced as "Mrs. Z.," whose lap was full of yarn.

Mrs. Blake invited us to have a seat, but I had just noticed a Siamese cat on the floor by the grandmother's feet. I plunked myself down in the middle of the room and patted my lap. The cat moved toward me, sniffed my outstretched hand, and then quickly nestled in the folds of my skirt, purring loudly.

"What's his name?" I asked.

"Joy," said Mrs. Blake. "She's my daughter Paula's cat." As if on cue, Paula came downstairs.

"Joy *loves* you," Paula said to me. She smiled. She was eighteen or nineteen, a college student, getting ready for fall semester. "You can keep her happy while I'm away," she told me.

I expected her mother to shoot her a look, for no one had told me I could stay here, yet. But Mrs. Blake was talking to my mother about her own husband's death from a heart attack a year before my father's. "It's so hard, but believe me you will get through it." The first anniversary had been terrible, she said. Now it was getting a little easier.

My mother nodded hopefully.

In September I moved to the happiest, best-run home I have known. Mrs. Blake was not a formal person after all, and never again did I see a look of forced neutrality on her face. When I mentioned our first meeting, she told me, "Oh, I didn't know what kind of girl you'd be. I didn't want to seem eager, in case you were somebody I wouldn't have in my house."

My bedroom was a corner room in a corner house, sunny and bright, with gabled windows that looked out on quiet streets below and over a small creek. If I leaned close to the panes, I could see a narrow bridge that led to a small shopping center. Only a dozen or so cars passed the house each day. There were trees along the creek, where birds sang late into the warm fall evenings.

Mrs. Z. was never without some needlework in her lap, and I was never without Joy in mine. Along with Mrs. Blake, we were the house's full-time residents. Student teachers would come for eight weeks and then leave, making room for others.

Paula was there for a few days when I moved in. She treated me with affection and my pregnancy with unabashed curiosity. "It's strange," she said, staring at my middle. "When you and your mother were here last week, you didn't look pregnant at all. Now you do."

I'd noticed it myself—a bulge in my abdomen—under the pink gingham babydoll dress that was finally out of the closet as a maternity smock. The bulge had appeared suddenly—instantly, in fact. The night before, I'd moved into the house with few belongings and not many clothes, since what I had wouldn't fit much longer. Mrs. Blake showed me to my room to unpack and then went downstairs to talk with my mother. I sat on the bed. Ahh, I breathed, allowing my shoulders to slump comfortably. As I relaxed, the waist on the same damn dress, as my mother called the one with the blue corn-flowers, suddenly felt tight. I unbuckled the belt. Unfastened the hook, the button. When I stood up to go back downstairs, I couldn't get the same damn dress fastened again. I put on the pink gingham.

"Why did you change?" my mother asked. She was writing out a check for Mrs. Blake.

"I just wanted to."

When Paula mentioned my bulge I shrugged. I was embarrassed that she had noticed. It was harder to be invisible here than it had been at home, where no one could stand to look at me anyway. Paula startled me by reaching out and putting her hand on my belly. "Aww," she murmured.

My mother visited a couple of evenings a week on her way home from work, or Saturday mornings. She didn't take me out, and I never left the house on my own, even for a short walk. I was like a toddler at day-care, who has learned to be away from her home comfortably only so long as she is in one particular substitute place. And anyway, I was hiding out. You don't leave your hideout—you might meet someone you know. The people we knew thought I was in Knoxville with my Aunt Irene, or at least that's what they were told.

I stayed indoors from morning to night, talking with Mrs. Blake in the kitchen, watching television with Mrs. Z. in the living room as she made a hooked rug for a great-grandchild, or reading in my bedroom. Since early childhood I had drawn and painted seriously, taking classes at the Corcoran Museum, in Washington, and with a private teacher in Arlington, and since my father's death I had drawn constantly, with unaccustomed focus, for in the act of putting marks on paper I had discovered I could empty my mind of everything but the changing page at my fingertips. So I had brought along pencils and pastels and a sheaf of paper to Mrs. Blake's. I found myself less inclined to work than I had predicted, but there were a few days when I did nothing but sketch Joy.

The rest of the time I thought about food.

At dinner in this peaceful tribe of girls and women, the student teachers asked me questions: "Are you afraid?" "Can you feel it kick?" And they teased me: "You must be faster than you look." For the first time in my life I felt comfortable in the role of little sister.

As a group, that fall, we cheered St. Louis during the World Series, damning the Yankees with contemptuous sneers. "Zat *awful* Vitey Vord!" Mrs. Z. spat, her heavy European accent giving new dimensions to the old, familiar names of American baseball players.

As a group, we hummed and moaned over Mrs. Blake's pork chop-and-scalloped-potato casserole. Pork roast with gravy. Roast beef with gravy. Chicken and gravy. Fresh green beans, fresh beets, fresh cranberry-orange relish, with roast turkey. And gravy. Stuffing with poultry, of course. And potatoes, sweet, baked, or new ones boiled and served with parsley butter. Rice, spiced in different ways and combined with sauteed onions. Bread and rolls—white, not whole wheat, and all home-baked—with butter. Night after night, dessert. Lemon meringue pie. Coconut cake. Chocolate cream pie.

Pecan pie. Devil's food cake. Mrs. Blake was splendid in her chosen line of work, as Casey Stengel said of Joe DiMaggio.

Every day I made myself a sandwich at lunchtime—something Mrs. Blake had negotiated with my mother—and that was the extent of my chores. At the other meals, I was served like a princess, one among several living in this two-story, red-brick, one-and-a-half-bath suburban palace. It was a relief to me, not so much from the grocery shopping and cooking I'd been doing at home, but from the make-believe adulthood I'd been simulating. I had been dazed by death and disgrace and exhausted by pregnancy, and it had been grueling to pull myself through each day. As soon as I was at Mrs. Blake's, the passive pleasures of infancy were restored to me. All was provided; nothing was expected. As a boarder in that warm womb, I could curl up, muster my strength, and wait.

I was also a junior in high school, however, so I had to keep up with classes. The Arlington County school system, in a gesture of remarkable enlightenment for the time, supplied tutors. Two or three days a week one of my teachers would arrive for a morning session at the dining room table.

I loved English and found it easy to read *Tender Is the Night* and write papers about ruined lives. Also, my English tutor, Mrs. Maurice, was a person I wanted to please. She looked like no one I'd ever met, with thick, flyaway, curly red hair, and she drove a sports car. Her "friend" had given it to her, she said. She brought me James Bond paperbacks to read when I wasn't reading Hemingway and Fitzgerald. They were full of sex—unzipped jumpsuits, heavy breathing, and the like—and I was flabbergasted. I didn't know that anyone wrote—let alone talked—about sex. And my stunning tutor not only talked about the sex in the books, she laughed about it.

At one point, Mrs. Maurice asked me what I knew about pregnancy. I shrugged. At her next visit, she gave me a different sort of book, *Childbirth Without Fear,* which I devoured. There was so much information in the world! Why didn't I know how to find any of it? One morning Mrs. Maurice told me about a friend whose water had broken while she was shopping on a crowded Saturday in Georgetown. I wasn't precisely sure what she meant—even with the book, I couldn't imagine what happened when your water broke, or why stylish M Street would be a bad site for that event. But I laughed along with Mrs. Maurice, trying to guess what this was all about.

A nervous note in her voice made me think that the story was about Mrs. Maurice herself, but she had never mentioned having a child, so I put that idea aside. Six years later, at a library in Washington, I saw her across the reading room standing with a little boy who looked to be about nine or ten. I ran up to say hello—I was in college then, and I had a million things I would have liked to tell her—but she smiled stiffly and put me off efficiently, leaving quickly with the little boy who might have been a baby whose birth began in Georgetown on a busy weekend. There had never been any mention of a Mr. Maurice. I wondered if this woman had been so kind to me because she had herself experienced something like my kind of pregnancy.

Mrs. Maurice also talked about art. She clicked her tongue when I told her I had come to love Matisse from looking at a reproduction in my eighth-grade French book. I described the painting to her— oranges in a bowl on a pink table with palm trees out the window. "The Egyptian Curtain," she said. I looked blank. "In the Phillips Collection." Blank again. "You've *never* been to the Phillips?"

She was aghast that someone who drew and painted as much as I did had never been to one of Washington's most treasured museums, so one rainy day she drove me to that perfect place, which was only twenty minutes from where I grew up.

We spent hours moving slowly from room to room. Behind a door I found a tiny Degas painting of a woman hugging herself tightly and leaning against the back of a settee. I believe it may be titled "Reflection," but when I first saw it I read the label as "Remorse," and for many years I thought of the painting with what I felt was special understanding.

After we left the Phillips, Mrs. Maurice took me to a Greek restaurant for baklava and then drove me to an open-air market, where farmers had set up produce stands. Far from the dimestore coffee counters and Safeway stores in Arlington, this world was urbane and seductive but also frighteningly unfamiliar to me.

When I mentioned the day's outing to my mother, she reacted with alarm. A neighbor of ours worked at the Phillips, she said. "What if he'd seen you? Just tell me, *what if he'd seen you?*"

"That woman!" my mother hissed, referring to Mrs. Maurice.

That woman was hard to resist. For one thing, she kept telling me I was smart—something only my father had said to me. It was intriguing—inspiring—and I hoped she wouldn't find out the truth. As it happened, she already knew. "You're completely disorganized. You don't know how to study," she said one day. "Your grades are going to be terrible."

As she harangued me, she changed the direction of my life. "You don't belong in the South. You don't have to settle for a Ford station wagon and a set of flatware," she would say. Mrs. Maurice listed New England women's colleges for me. "Well, you'd never get into my alma mater—Smith—but why don't you try Wheaton or Connecticut College for Women? They might take you because of your high SAT scores." I hadn't taken the SATs yet.

Dan, meanwhile, wrote to me often from boot camp. His letters described the beautiful children we would someday create together, including "a little girl with pigtails."

I winced, but I could not begin to probe my traitorous feelings. Dan was waiting for me to graduate from high school so that we could marry. I appeared to collaborate with him; I even thought I was in agreement about our future. Subconsciously, however, I was making other plans.

I wrote to my best friend, Louise, in Germany, to tell her what was happening to me. As she still does, she wrote me back a long, warm letter. Her friendship, with its unquestioning love, was my only connection to a way of life—one that included friends and shared confidences—that had ended for me in 1963. I wrote to one or two other friends as well, but not to anyone whose parents were close friends of my mother's, in case they told. None of them answered.

Dan wrote to me almost every day. I have only two or three of his letters now. In one he says that he doesn't know what to feel, now that I am no longer leaning on him. He can only feel strong, he says, when I need him. He apologizes profusely, abjectly, for insisting on having sex at some point before his enlistment. He says he knew I didn't want to. He promises never to do that again.

Life was quiet at Mrs. Blake's. I ate and sat and drew and struggled to study. The baby grew and began to kick. Joy, always purring, found ingenious new ways to wrap herself around the obstruction in my lap.

One cold, gray December day I was sitting on my bed when I looked out the window and saw the new Mustang. The driver paused at a stop sign at the end of the bridge, then rolled through it, easing left, in the direction of the house.

I had grown up around boys who knew a '56 Chevy from a '57. They might use their father's trim little Tempest to take a girl out the first few times, when it was important to make a good impression, and then switch to the family Rambler wagon, whose seats dropped back, when they decided it was time to get to know her better. Although I was in advanced-placement classes at school, the kids I knew best, the kids in my neighborhood, were not dreaming of acing the Merit Scholarship test. The boy next door, whose father was a building contractor, had spent his adolescence messily dismantling a red Sprite in his driveway, to the dismay of some of our house-proud neighbors. Now, at sixteen, he made $25 an hour after school as a mechanic in a foreign-car garage.

I scrutinized the Mustang as it came my way, feeling a brief tightness in my chest as I watched it go by. It was love at first sight, but I suppressed it, imagining that I would never again hang around someone's gravel driveway listening to boys my age expound on the negligible advantages of the Plymouth slant-six engine while I nervously touched my hair to check my flip. The Mustang passed by. I was intoxicated by its tropical color, while at the same time uneasily aware that a hibiscus-hued vehicle was not in what my mother and her friends would consider good taste. In every way, the car was beyond my ken.

Slowly, I lay down, arranging my stomach so that its swelling form neither pinched nor pressed, and patted the bedspread for Joy to come and curl up with me. Together, we napped until dinnertime.

The isolating, introspective nature of pregnancy was accentuated for me by my real loneliness and furthered by the denial—mine and almost everyone else's—that seemed to surround me. My late pregnancy was taking place in a bizarre vacuum of silence. Of the people with whom I came into regular contact, only Mrs. Maurice talked with me frankly about it.

With the advantage of hindsight I sometimes wish that I had gone to the Crittenden Home, where I could have compared my experiences, and my feelings, with those of other girls. In *Wake Up Little Susie,* Rickie Solinger wrote that

for most [of the girls and young women], the maternity home offered the opportunity for a collective experience in which the girls together built a spirit of elan, humor, and hope. One director remarked, 'They get along astonishingly well together, considering that they are often from many different social and economic levels.' When a group of unwed mothers in a home were asked, 'What is your opinion about living with a group of girls sharing the same experience. . . . ?' one of the most common answers was positive because 'everyone is equal.' The leveling experience of single pregnancy meant that status differences that had meaning outside and would have separated girls from each other were meaningless in the home. The girls were defined inside, as outside, by their pregnancy, but inside, it could be a source of sharing, solidarity, and inspiration.

I have since met birth mothers who went into homes. For some it was a positive experience, the secrecy tempered by camaraderie. For others, it was far, far worse than my hideout at Mrs. Blake's. In almost all of the homes, the women gave birth without any close friend or relative to comfort them. Some were treated with sympathy, some with condescension, and some with open contempt. When I recently read Solinger's remarkable book on the era, I was not surprised to read about the pronounced differences in care for black or white pregnant women: It was nearly impossible for a black woman to find a home where she could live safely, privately, and with comparative dignity while awaiting the birth of her child. Also, black babies were harder to place for adoption. Many black mothers kept their children for those reasons alone, but Solinger also found evidence of a general reluctance on the part of black families to give up the babies of their unmarried daughters. "You give away puppies, not children," said one grandmother bluntly.

As I bring my own experience to the forefront of my consciousness, in order to write about it, what emerges is, above all, an overwhelming sense of loneliness. I felt at the time, and for many years afterward, that no one could possibly understand what I had gone through, and that even if they did they wouldn't care.

One afternoon before Christmas, my mother took me out to do some shopping. (I later wrapped the gifts, addressed the packages, and sent them to Aunt Irene to mail from Knoxville.) While we were in a department store, carrying shopping bags and wearing our heavy winter coats, a clerk seemed to take extra pains to help us. I hardly noticed him. I hardly noticed anything any more. As he turned aside to ring up our bill, Mother smiled and whispered to me, "He's *flirting* with you!" I was mortified that I'd been noticed. I turned and walked away, ostensibly to look at a rack of clothes, knowing Mother was stuck there to pay. "What is the *matter* with you?" she said when she caught up with me. "Can't you just be nice to people?"

Dan earned a pass to come home for a week during the holidays. The morning he was to arrive, I could not sit still. I felt sick with anticipation. To distract myself, I offered to help Mrs. Z., so she took me down to the basement to check some fruitcakes that she had baked for friends. She basted them regularly with brandy; this time she had forgotten to bring the baster. "Vait here," she said, as she went back up to the kitchen to get it. I was sitting at the bottom of the dimly lit stairs when I thought I heard a gasp. Then another and another, exactly like the rhythmic, agonized breaths my father had struggled to take as he lay dying of the heart attack.

I raced up the stairs, trying to avoid kicking my stomach with my knees. There was Mrs. Z., looking in a drawer for the baster, and Mrs. Blake, icing a cake by turning the cake plate with one hand and wielding a spatula in the other. The plate scraped the tile counter: *scrape,* stroke, *scrape,* stroke. I burst into a flood of tears—the only ones I had cried for nearly a year.

"You *are* a mess," said Mrs. Blake, putting her arms around me. I told her what had happened, and she finished the cake without once making the rasping sound. "I'll never do *that* again," she said.

Dan came over that evening to take me out. We exchanged gifts. I do not remember what I gave him. He brought me a string of pearls, which he had bought at the PX on his navy base. I have them still. Although they are real cultured pearls, the beads are mismatched and cloudy. When I opened the long, dark blue box and saw them, I made the proper happy sounds, but I hated putting them on.

Dan drove to a fancy restaurant in Baltimore, where we would be sure not to see anyone who might recognize us. It took an hour and a half to get there, and when we arrived the maitre d' blinked once and led us to a small, dark table next to the noisy kitchen doorway.

There we sat, a pregnant sixteen-year-old girl in a homemade maternity smock and a boy in full-dress navy uniform, pretending to enjoy our expensive meal. Perhaps Dan did, in fact, enjoy it. I was humiliated by the second-rate pearls and the back-alley table. It would have taken breakfast at Tiffany's to persuade me of my worth.

On the way home to Mrs. Blake's, Dan drove the car to a secluded overlook on the George Washington Memorial Parkway. He hurriedly tilted the front seat down, and we leaned back. I was eight months pregnant. The baby pressed so hard on my diaphragm that I could hardly breathe, but Dan seemed oblivious to my gasping discomfort. I told him I had to go back. Romance was no longer possible. Its result was now literally, as well as figuratively, oppressive to me.

3

The representative white unwed mother—the one described by academic studies, government officials, agency personnel, and the media as typical—was, in general, broadly middle class, in the sense that she was perceived as having parents who could and would, in her behalf, negotiate with helping institutions and underwrite their daughter's care. She had, despite her unfortunate sexual misstep, the likely potential to become a wife and mother in the postcrisis phase of her life. And most important, she was in the process of producing a white baby of value on the postwar adoption market.

Rickie Solinger, *Wake Up Little Susie*

ONE DAY, sitting in Mrs. Blake's living room, I decided to waive my rights to a court notification of adoption in order to allow my baby-to-be to be placed immediately in an adoptive home. This way, the baby would not have to go to a foster home for a waiting period until I was notified of the adoption, at which time I could either give my consent or withdraw it. That was what I was told.

When I decided to sign the waiver, the look on the pleasant face of the social worker from the Winnicott Foundation was so much like the look I had seen on the face of Dan's father when I said I would give the baby up that I actually hesitated. Was I doing this for the social worker? It was beginning to seem that whenever I extracted myself from a situation, the result was a satisfied look on the face of an adult.

I do remember that it seemed abundantly clear to me that I would never reclaim the baby. It seemed the height of selfishness to consign a newborn to a foster home when if I only signed a waiver he or she could go directly to the wonderful home with the wonderful parents who were older, married, educated, and well off—who were in every way better than I was.

I don't remember a thing the pleasant lady from Winnicott ever said to me or anything I said to her. I don't remember any other meeting with her. If I was given counseling, and I surely was, for Winnicott was a responsible agency, I have no memory of it. Unlike Mrs. Maurice, the Winnicott woman made no dent in my general unconsciousness. But then, her job was not the one that Mrs. Maurice seemed to have taken on: to assure me that I would not always be vague, depressed, and thoroughly incompetent. To remind me of my strengths and to suggest that they were admirable and worth considering as I stumbled on in life.

Perhaps it wasn't possible to offer me real therapy. I'd refused that once before, after I'd sliced my wrist and my mother offered to take me to my sister's psychiatrist. In any case the only counseling I remember came from Mrs. Maurice, who shrugged at my pregnancy, looked to the future, and told me, in countless direct and indirect ways, that I was an intelligent, valuable person who deserved respect. It was a message I would need to hear again and again, for two decades, before I would be able to incorporate it as part of my own view of myself. I thought of myself as stupid, careless, and contemptible, and I had no sympathy for such a person, who had brought misery not only upon myself but on two families as well. It was easy to believe that a child could have no worse start in life than to be born to a mother like me. The baby's only hope was to go to someone else as quickly as possible and be spared any further contamination.

"It will be easier to give up the baby if she doesn't see it," the obstetrician assured my mother. We were sitting in his office, Mother straight across the desk from him, me back a little and to one side.

Perhaps because I was so young, perhaps because he was embarrassed by my condition and what it implied, or perhaps simply because my mother was paying his bill, the doctor spoke always to her, rarely to me. My mother would drive me to my appointments, sit in the waiting room until the pelvic examination was over, and then come in when the doctor was seated behind his desk. I was their audience, listening as they worked out their plans. This particular visit took place in winter.

I had been coming to this office since summer, doing whatever I was told but basically aiming for an out-of-body experience, one that would enable me to transcend my corporeal self while the visit lasted. Especially during the pelvic exam. Astonishing! It seemed grossly, flagrantly wanton.

I was so acutely embarrassed that I kept my eyes closed throughout. There is a term, "conservation of objects," that child-development specialists use to describe the achievement of a very young baby who learns that even when an object is not in view, it nonetheless still exists. In this doctor's office, I tried to back up to the point in early infancy when what was not visible had no reality. When I closed my eyes and clenched my teeth (so tightly that one tense morning I broke a molar), it was my intention that the examining table disappear, that the stirrups dissolve, that my legs, no longer seen by me behind the sheet, were somewhere other than up in the air, and that the doctor and nurse were less than figments.

It never worked. But the examination would end, and I would survive to sit in the third chair, listening to my mother and the doctor discuss my case.

"The second semester at her school starts in February," my mother said anxiously, that winter day.

The doctor nodded calmly and flipped through his desk calendar. "Let's see. If she's late, January fifteenth is good. We'll induce. That way you won't have the uncertainty."

"January fifteenth?" My mother wrote the date on a slip of paper, using her purse to steady it. "January fifteenth. Do we—"

The doctor held up his hand. "I'll give you the particulars when it's time."

My mother did not put the paper in her purse, or reach behind her for her coat, or make any gesture of understanding that the interview was ending. She was always slightly paralyzed, slightly stricken at these appointments. My betrayal—of decency, of common sense, of *her*—added immensely to the weight of grief that slowed her movements and made it difficult for her to leave the office of this authoritative, sympathetic man. She had lost her husband and needed someone to lean on, and this man was not a bad choice, though his support was necessarily brief and intermittent.

"Soon, you can put it all behind you," he said to her. And then, as if in afterthought, he looked at me benignly and nodded. "And so can you."

Here I sit, a middle-aged woman in another winter, thirty years later, waiting for the day when I can put it all behind me.

As my body became larger, even I began to ignore it. I would shower without glancing down. When, one day, I accidentally caught a glimpse of myself in a mirror, I was shocked to see blue lines radiating out from my nipples and across my breasts. The fissures looked like deep scars. When I had my next doctor's appointment, I anxiously asked him how long it would take them to go away after the birth.

"Why, those won't go away!" he said with a snort. "Those are stretch marks! They're permanent!"

His forthright answer startled me. I blinked, but I quietly looked away and forced myself not to cry. I hadn't realized there would be visible scars. I had been told, again and again, that I would give my baby up and *put this all behind me*. How could that happen if I, like Hester Prynne with her scarlet A, bore the sign of my disgrace forever? The doctor might have told me that the marks would lighten and fade, that they might be but barely visible after a time, but he did not.

On January 15, 1965, my mother drove me to Fairfax Hospital, in a neighboring county, to have the birth induced.

Upon entering the hospital I was put in a wheelchair. My passivity in the entire process of pregnancy was now an enforced state, as I was put to bed and hooked up to an IV.

I began to feel cramping almost immediately. I remembered what *Childbirth Without Fear* had said about breathing, and I tried to take deep, easing gulps of air. At one point, my legs were spread by nurses. Someone lanced the amniotic sac, and I felt a rush of warm liquid. I know that now, but at the time thought I had lost control of my bladder, and I was sick with embarrassment. As the nurses changed the towels on which I had been resting they seemed unfazed by this accident.

I forgot whatever I'd read about contractions almost as soon as the pains started, but I was determined not to cry or complain. It is probably a small failure of later therapy and especially of my own insight that I still cannot quite say why stoicism seemed the only acceptable route for me then.

During the long day, I was put in a labor room with other women. Those women moaned. They screamed. They thrashed in their beds. They looked demented.

"Please make them stop!," I begged my doctor. "I can't stand listening to them!"

"They don't know they're doing it," the doctor answered. All the women were in "twilight sleep." Soon I would be in it too: drugged to the point where only intense pain could rouse me, so that the contractions seemed to come one on top of another, without stopping. There were periods of rest, of course, but we were out for those. All we were able to experience was the pain, and it was severe. I was shocked that my body could feel such agony. I was panic-stricken. I thought I was coming apart—that the searing, shooting, tearing pains were literally splitting me to pieces. There was no one to whom I felt I could tell my fears. After a while I could no longer speak, even when I was awake during a contraction.

Would I die? I wanted to know if my mother was still in the hospital, so I could see her one last time. I was suddenly sure that I did not want to die. On the other hand, it might be preferable to this. I wanted to tell the doctor to find my mother for me, but when

I opened my eyes I could only stare at him beseechingly.

He looked back at me with a calm that seemed utterly inappropriate.

I heard a long, low moan. As I tried to tell the doctor to make the woman stop, I recognized my own voice.

"I'm still pregnant!"

Those were my first words, when I finally awoke in a dark room late that evening. I was shocked that my abdomen was still large. I thought I would be a size 8 again within minutes of the birth.

I remembered my mother telling me that the baby was a boy and weighed seven pounds, six ounces. Two and a half decades later, Laura weighed seven pounds, six ounces. When my obstetrician called out her weight, I jumped. But there was another coincidence in my son's birth that strikes me as more important. I discovered it only recently, perusing a book about pregnancy and birth that gave due dates to correspond to conception dates. Moving my finger from the date I thought I had conceived, I calculated that my first baby had been due on my father's birthday. Had I subconsciously contrived to produce a new version of my beloved father, gone forever? Many years later *Time* magazine reported on a study that found a significant correlation between paternal death and a teenage daughter's illegitimate pregnancy.

My stay in the hospital was a little longer, I believe, than it would have been for another new mother. I wasn't really a new mother, anyway. From the moment I awoke I was straining to return to being a teenager, straining even as I lay in the hospital bed to concentrate on the future. This was the future in which I would be restored, like new. I would then get on with my life—after this mistake was cleared up and the slate, to say nothing of my body, was wiped clean.

I couldn't stand up without fainting. The nurses, who soon realized they had to be at my side whenever I attempted to rise from the bed, were kind or indifferent or contemptuous. I waited, each day, for the one in the morning who always said, as she lifted me up off the floor after another blackout, "Poor thing, poor thing. You're just a baby yourself." When the head nurse came to examine my perineum, she asked me to turn on my side, bend my knees, and draw my hospital gown away from my backside. Even though I could not see her face, and even though she said only, "You may want to soak in a warm tub," I thought I felt her revulsion. I assumed it was because I was an unwed teenage mother. I myself felt an identical loathing.

When from time to time over the years I have recalled my memory of that hospital stay, I have been appalled by the hurt, both physical and psychological, which I was able, then, to bear stoically, without shedding a single tear.

No, wait. I forgot. I shed buckets of them.

After the birth, I was placed on the maternity ward, but I was given a private room at the very end of the long hall. I kept my door shut most of the time and did not once leave my room during the seven days I was kept in the hospital. I was afraid of seeing the babies. One morning I heard someone open my door, and when I looked over, expecting one of the nurses, there was a bassinet at the threshold of my room. Apparently someone had stopped the person who was about to wheel it to my bedside. "No!" I cried, though it was already being pulled back.

I heard my own voice as if I were listening to a conversation in the next room. My reaction was far from the feelings I actually had, such as curiosity, and something like love.

Baby-love is a congenital condition, I think, and probably has little to do with the rest of motherhood. Babies have always seemed familiar to me, not mysterious. They seem understandable. I love them when I pick them up, and they seem to sense that. Normally, I would have leapt for a bassinet. But this was not *any* baby. This baby was evidence. This baby was the only crack in the attenuated edifice of lies and denial that sustained me. Without the baby, I soon would appear to be a normal girl having a normal life.

The doctor had said again and again that I should not see the baby. In a book called *The Art of Adoption,* author Linda Cannon Burgess, an adoption-agency social worker, mentioned a call she received from a birth mother who wanted to know more about her child, whom she, too, had never laid eyes on. Burgess surmised, "If with love she had held and blessed her child, she could then have surrendered her for adoption without the burden of future guilt." I want to meet the mother who held her baby, relinquished him, and escaped that guilt. As Jan Waldron, a birth mother who spent sixteen days with her newborn daughter, wrote in her beautiful memoir, *Giving Away Simone,* "In the year after I gave my daughter away, I fought the pull to reclaim her every heart-pounding second of every day. . . . I thought if I could just see and touch her I could wake up one day and go on. But seeing her would have unhinged me. I had made a deal that felt less like a promise than a pathetic default. . . . But I did not call."

In a 1988 article in the *New York Times Magazine* titled "Chosen and Given," Robin Marantz Henig wrote, "A generation ago, few experts recognized what is now seen as one inescapable fact of adoption: it is a psychological burden to the adoptee." She quoted a nine-year-old boy who referred to "the master question of my life—why was I given up for adoption?" And she interviewed a psychotherapist and the adoptive mother of two children, who said, "For many, there's always a sadness about it. As a parent, I feel an additional burden knowing Sam and Molly have a pain, and will carry that pain all their lives."

When I read the article the first time, I felt a miserable combination of sorrow and guilt. When I read it more recently, I was struck by the thought that if birth mothers carry a lifelong ache, and if adoptees are similarly afflicted, then for whom is this adoption business designed? (I have been asked if I've given any thought to the plight of those who are childless and yearn for parenthood. I have. I was childless and yearned to be a mother for nearly twenty-five years, from age sixteen to age forty-one. I was also fatherless, from the age of fifteen, but I would not take someone else's father, even if I was assured that I was welcome to do so.)

What if I had been told, You can keep your child and stay at Mrs. Blake's house, until you finish college and can take care of yourself? Would I have made a different choice? I was a pretty disturbed teenager who needed to build her life back up, but *I was also a mother*. Would it have been possible for someone like Mrs. Blake to be paid foster-parent wages to keep us both, me and the baby, as is done in some Scandinavian countries?

It is a complicated situation. I wish I knew what was right. There is a movement now towards "family preservation" wherever it is possible. Its proponents believe that children, ideally, should remain with their biological kin. I wish I believed that, absolutely. But I don't—not absolutely. I can't force myself to think that adoption is *always* a mistake. But neither do I believe *absolutely* that adoption is the right route, even for a young pregnant girl with no resources. In other words, I can never be absolutely sure that the choice I made was the right one.

When I was in my late twenties, my mother mentioned a friend who'd had a difficult birth. "She tore a lot," she told me. "She had to have sixteen stitches." I looked at her blankly for a second, sensing some buried knowledge tugging at my mental sleeve. And then I remembered. As I had lain in my bed the day after the birth, the doctor had said to a nurse, "She'll need some iron, and a painkiller." To me he said, "It took sixty-five stitches to sew you up," with a hint of pride, as if I might want to boast about it later. When the head nurse examined me, she probably recoiled not from my ignominy but from the sight of bruised and swollen flesh.

Sitting with my mother on a rare visit home, long after I had been to college and moved away forever, it was difficult for me to reconstruct the scene, difficult to dredge up the memory of it at all. I had dissociated myself from the experience soon after the birth, rather than feel it—any of it—and suffer.

At first my emotional dislocation took the form of contempt, but beginning in my late twenties, I was old enough to allow some sympathy to emerge. Still thoroughly disconnected from my own emotions I would think of the one who had lain on that bed too weak to walk, too weak at first even to raise her head, as "that poor little girl." As if it had not been me.

PART TWO

A Nice Girl Like Me

4

I was not counseled. I was not comforted.
Carol Schaefer, *The Other Mother*

I RETURNED HOME from the hospital, not to Mrs. Blake's, of course, but to my mother's house. I walked gingerly from the car to the front door. The ground was covered with an inch-and-a-half of snow, and I remember being afraid I would slip and fall. Can it be that every day was overcast that winter? This one, like so many others I remember, was colorless, shadowless, dim. Home did not look welcoming. Even under the unifying, if threadbare, blanket of whiteness, the yard had a dreary, neglected look. A broken limb from a poplar tree lay where it had blown down. Fall leaves were rotting in a tangle of brambles by the creek.

Slowly I made my way along the shoveled walk, taking small steps until I reached the front stoop. Once inside, I was struck by a sense of decay, disorder, and depression. The kitchen counters seemed not to have been washed in the five months I'd been gone, the linoleum floor was unwaxed and dull, the white organdy curtains in my bedroom windows were gray and limp. Dust kittens curled in the corners.

At first there was nothing I could do but spend my days on the couch or in bed. I was still in some physical pain that second week. (I was adept, by now, at keeping my emotional pain at bay.) I could walk, but not easily. I could sit, but only if I held my breath, and I still became faint when I stood.

My sister was living at home, too, but we ignored one another during those years. As if she were only a curious neighbor, Sally was told the current version of my story: that I was recovering from a back injury at Aunt Irene's. No one who heard the story asked for details.

In the hospital, I had been given an injection to stop lactation, but one of my breasts filled up with milk anyway and remained swollen, red, and burning hot for two days. At first, I was terrified. I ran to my mother's room in the middle of the night, once more afraid that a part of me was going to explode.

"It's just your milk coming in!" she said, with the angry note of exasperation that told me I'd forced her out of her own defensive cocoon of not-knowing. "Go back to bed!"

School was out for semester break. I had a while to recuperate. One day, I woke up feeling miraculously better, and the next day I felt actually good. I took down the curtains in my bedroom and washed them in the laundry sink, where the water instantly turned black.

I remembered that after my father died, I had thought that it was up to me to be strong. I had no faith in my mother's ability to cope with everyday life. The state of the house confirmed my unhappy suspicion that someone needed to take charge, and that the only someone who was even minimally aware of how much needed doing was me. I now think of myself as disorganized, distracted, and even dim, especially about matters of housekeeping, but when I look back I realize that my mother, for the rest of her life, frequently relied on me as if I were level-headed and capable, and so I tried hard to be those things. Faking competence, I sometimes surprised myself by achieving it.

I went into a feverish spell of activity, an almost manic phase, rushing from place to place. I had a similar spell after Laura was born. I suffered, I said, from post-partum elation—the precise opposite of the depression that often strikes new mothers. In 1965 it took the form not of happiness but of determined, spirited energy. I scrubbed counters, scoured floors, and cleaned out drawers. I gathered the trash, sorted the mail, stacked and bundled old magazines and newspapers and advertisements. I threw out food from the refrigerator that I vaguely recognized from the previous September. I was appalled at how my mother was living. And, too, it was a relief to shake myself out with the dustmop, to move so fast no grief could catch me.

"You make me tired," my mother said.

One afternoon the neighbor with the mechanic son came over to welcome me back. I was wearing a forest-green cardigan and a plaid kilt with a waistband I'd easily loosened by moving two buttons. Mrs. A. sat on the couch. My mother and I sat in armchairs. As we talked, Mrs. A. glanced at me compassionately.

I couldn't seem to stop fiddling with the buttons on the sweater just below my waist. Button. Unbutton. Button. Unbutton. I was vaguely conscious of what I was doing, and I remember thinking it was a weird sort of tic to develop.

Mrs. A. left to go home, after hugging me tightly and whispering "Poor Peggy."

My mother turned to me furiously. "What the hell were you doing with that sweater?" she demanded. "Do you want people to guess? What is the *matter* with you?"

I was playing with the buttons near the site of my sorrow. And yet for a long time, the closure of my son's utterly closed adoption was useful to me, for it freed me to grow up at my own fairly slow pace. Would my psychological growth have progressed a bit faster if I'd been allowed to live the truth, to be known in my world as a birth mother? I wonder what would have happened if I had seen my child and relinquished him with some sense of the importance of what I was doing, and not within a charade of normalness that was meant to suggest that my life could go on as it had before it was shattered.

It was shattered.

I think a lot about abortion—about safe, legal abortion, which was not available to me. I think about sex education, and what that should mean. I think about the complex emotions that surround sex for a young girl. Why is sex such a powerful draw for some, but not, apparently, for others? What makes it so difficult to resist, for some? I think that if either Dan or I had received reliable information about contraceptives—if we had even been able to buy condoms—I might not have become pregnant. Or if we had been able to go to Planned Parenthood when we first knew I was pregnant, I could have had a safe, legal abortion, with minimal interruption of my young life.

My friend Susan, the obstetrician, has been under pressure from her hospital's board of directors and from various doctors at her hospital solely because of her pro-choice convictions. She is one of the few obstetricians in business for more than fifteen years who has never had a malpractice suit brought against her. She is so superior a physician that her malpractice insurance costs are half the average. And yet because she performs abortions, she has been forced to bring a lawsuit against her hospital in order to keep practicing. Otherwise, the anti-choice board would shut her out.

One surgeon at the hospital who had been particularly active against Susan recently brought his pregnant girlfriend in to her office and paid for the woman's abortion. When he went back to his anti-choice activities, Susan's husband, in an uncharacteristic moment of frustration and rage, screamed "Hypocrite!" at him in the hospital parking lot. The surgeon smiled.

Susan does not go a day without wondering if this is the day she should put on a helmet and a bulletproof vest. Susan is the mother of two children. She worries about exposing herself and her family to danger. Should she stay where she is, in a small town, where she stands out? Or should she move to a city, where she would be less alone—less of a target? Susan is a Quaker, so at meeting she prayed to God for clarity. "And God answered my prayer," she told me. "He said, 'Build a rec room.'" We both laughed at this, but Susan understood the deeper message: Stay. Be a witness for your beliefs.

To me, the Susans of the medical world are the guardian angels of desperate girls and women.

> So, to their unutterable torment, they go about among their fellow-creatures, looking pure as new-fallen snow while their hearts are all speckled and spotted with iniquity of which they cannot rid themselves.
> Nathaniel Hawthorne, *The Scarlet Letter*

In school, I was cut off from my peers. I had been altered, first by my father's death and then by my pregnancy, and I could not seem to re-enter the world of classes and church choirs and weekend dances, much as I wanted to. I was nothing like the "good" girls who studied and joined clubs that performed community service. Nor was I like the girls who in those days were called "fast," who seemed to be enjoying themselves and hoping their luck would hold. I was brokenhearted.

Some of my teachers could not bring themselves to look at me, but there was one, Mr. Shelton, who shook my hand, and told me he was delighted to have me in his class. As if my return to school were not hard enough, the first book studied in the second semester of junior English was *The Scarlet Letter*. Mr. Shelton smiled encouragingly in my direction several times a day, but he did not call on me to speak on any subject until we had moved on to another text.

By spring I must have felt better, for I went along with a new friend when she decided to try out for cheerleading. Week after week, I joined the ranks of the pretty-enough in the gym after school, where we bounced and yelled until we were sweaty and hoarse. I could do a terrific airborne leap, my toes nearly touching the back of my head. Several of the cheerleader-coaches predicted I'd be chosen.

The afternoon of the tryouts, I waited in the bleachers for my turn. There were five teachers seated at a long table at one end of the gymnasium.

My name was called. I walked to the center of the gleaming floor. A teacher who wore chopsticks in her hair gave the signal, and I began to do my stuff.

In practice I had smiled and even laughed as we would-a-beens had gone through the ridiculous motions together, but suddenly I could not for the life of me use the muscles in my face to raise the corners of my mouth. The teacher-judges, looking as uncomfortable as I felt, saw a trim, strong teenager leaping and yelling with all her might, but with a grim expression on her knowing face.

What was it that I knew? I knew that as a happy-looking girl I was a fraud. An infinitesimal part of me also knew that I was too smart for this nonsense. In my reduced state, that inkling led not to self-respect, as it might well have, but to the simpler certainty that I just did not belong.

I was invited to speak with a guidance counselor. She was a very large woman, perfectly groomed, firmly girdled. She spoke reassuringly, sympathetically, trying to draw me out as she offered herself as a possible confidante. As she talked, she shifted her bulk in her chair. She tugged at the hem of her skirt. She picked up and put down the papers on her desk. She touched her hair repeatedly, stroking every strand into place. Nothing in her manner seemed condescending, but like so many of those around me who were nominally adults, she was clearly uncomfortable in my presence.

I was patient with her, but I would have none of her comforting. At one point I was moved to speak of "people like me" with contempt. I can't remember my remark, but the gist of it was that pregnant teenagers didn't deserve sympathy; that their dilemma was their own fault.

She reddened. She kept talking, trying valiantly to give me a second chance to accept her kindness. Her offer, I am sure, was intended to help me "put it all behind me." I'd been hearing about that for so long—from the Winnicott Foundation social worker, from the obstetrician, from Dan's parents, from my mother—that I thought I would scream if I had to hear it again.

The other part of my problem was that if I accepted this woman's words of encouragement, I would have started to cry. Once I started, I might cry forever. To continue to live inside my skin, I needed the shell of my self-contempt to protect me from everything I knew—especially from my despair.

Twenty-one years later, after my mother's death, I noticed that there were days when I could function only if no one said a caring word to me. When my good friends looked at me with love and expressed their sincere sympathy and offered to help me, I broke down. But whereas those breakdowns as an adult (with years of therapy under my belt) were sad, they were not debilitating. At thirty-seven, I had an inner strength that enabled me, after I cried, to get back to work, do my job, get on with ordinary life.

At sixteen, I was a mollusk. For me, the shell was everything.

Dan completed the six-month navy basic training and returned home. He went to work as a government messenger in order to repay my mother $400, half the cost of my pregnancy.

There we were: two teenagers living in their parents' houses less than a block apart in a lovely suburb. I did not return to church, although I missed singing in the choir. It no longer made sense to me to raise a joyful noise unto the Lord.

Dan and I usually saw each other in the evening, always at my house. He would bring me flowers—usually blue bachelor buttons, for which I must have expressed a preference—or some other small token of affection. I received these gifts with delight. Dan himself I received with something like tolerance, though I pretended that I was in love with him and that I still intended to marry him someday.

My performance lacked conviction. One warm spring evening, he appeared at the screen door without his customary offering. I don't know if I forgot the warm-and-welcoming smile altogether or if there was simply a telling hesitation between his arrival and my greeting, but Dan looked at me and said, "Sometimes I think you don't want to see me if I don't bring you a present."

I didn't want to see him even if he did, but flowers made it easier for me to pull off my charade.

Now that I see in my husband the type of humorous, outgoing, sociable man that I love, I can also see that there was precious little possibility that Dan and I would ever have clicked. Dan was something of an isolationist; I seemed to be enough for him. He didn't like meeting new people, he said. I didn't argue with Dan. He was strongly built, and when his temper flared he shouted. But I had grown up in a crowd of neighborhood children; although I now felt set apart from normal life, I wistfully remembered what it had been like to be part of a larger community.

Driving home to our neighborhood on the way back from Washington, where we sometimes went on dates, there was a particular left turn for which I always braced myself. Dan would recklessly cut the corner and turn left into the oncoming lane of the side street. Sitting next to him on the front seat, in the days before seat belts, I would stiffen my arm, press a hand against the dashboard, and grit my teeth. He would insist angrily that he was in complete control.

The street was winding and hilly, with poor visibility. The little brother of a friend of mine had been killed by a car there the year before. There were new stop signs and often police parked nearby. I hoped Dan would be ticketed for his crazy shortcut, but he was never caught.

"Dan always cut to the left of that," I said to my mother as we drove back from the pool one evening several summers later. I pointed to the stop sign at the dangerous turn.

"*What?*" she said, her voice high, alarmed.

"He would swoop around the left side, so he wouldn't have to slow down so much."

By then it was in the past; I remembered it vaguely; I spoke of it desultorily. But my mother gripped the dash, pulled herself upright and tightened her lips. She demanded to know why I hadn't told her this years before. "I *never* would have let you go out with him if I'd known he was that kind of driver!"

My mother's point of view struck me even then as unbalanced, but I know it is not always easy for parents to keep their perspective.

My friend Jill's father was a dentist. One morning, one of his patients—like him the father of a teenage daughter—asked if Jill was on the pill.

"Hmm?" murmured Jill's father absentmindedly, as he waited for the man to rinse, spit, and lean back.

"When my daughter turned thirteen," the patient explained, "I started putting a birth-control pill in her coffee every morning."

"*What?*" said Jill's father, horrified. "You give *coffee* to a thir*teen*-year-old?"

Did Dan and I kiss that spring? Did we neck? Did we pet? I can't remember a thing, except Dan holding my feet for me while I lay on the living room floor doing sit-ups to tighten my already flat-again stomach. And apparently we took photographs of one another. Until recently I had dozens of them stored away with other childhood mementos. Whenever I came across them, over the years, I averted my eyes. Finally, in 1990, I dropped them down the incinerator chute of my New York apartment building. They were pleasant, sunny, and cheerful pictures, with both of us smiling and clowning for the camera. More lies.

During the summer, just before my senior year in high school, Dan was ready to begin college. His choice was, as it had been the year before, between a university in the Midwest and a college in Maryland. Dan had a positive gift for putting geographical distance between himself and me, and he chose the one in the Midwest.

He was simply choosing the better school, he said.

I looked at Dan. Although I no longer loved him, I depended on his presence. I needed a boyfriend, and he was the one I had. I needed someone, and he was the someone I had. And he was the only person my age who knew what I had been through. This time, however, I did not plead with him to stay. This time I spoke as clearly and simply as I could: "Stay nearby. That way we can see each other."

He went anyway. I have to keep reminding myself that he was seventeen, eighteen—a boy. That he hardly deserves my continuing, bitter disappointment. That he, like me, was at the mercy of a complicated life that necessarily, because of our youth, included parents. I remember that the midwestern school was much cheaper, and I think that was one deciding factor.

Later on, I was glad that Dan made his choice and stuck by it despite my explicit request. It made it easier, ultimately, to break up with him. As it was, I felt trapped in a suffocating relationship that I valued for only the vaguest, most desperate reasons. Worse, it was a relationship to which I felt I owed allegiance. I owed Dan love because I'd given away his baby. I owed him loyalty because he'd been loyal to me, albeit not at close range.

I wonder if Dan thought I also owed him sex; I was hardly a virgin any more. Whatever he thought about me, he was always interested in sex. Apparently he was not traumatized by our experience, as I was. But then, the experience had been mostly mine.

During the summer I was invited to join Dan's family on a vacation to the Maine coast, near a rocky shore where I swam in a pink gingham two-piece bathing suit, my vertical, teenage tummy a wonder of rejuvenation. My stretch-marked breasts didn't show under the modest, gathered top. No one could have imagined my swollen figure eight months before.

I shared a room with Dan's sisters in a remote white house on an old farm surrounded by acres of ancient orchards. Someone had brought a .22 rifle, and one afternoon Dan taught me how to shoot.

I held up the gun and squinted into the sight. My contact lens didn't fit right, and I couldn't see well, but I pulled the trigger anyway. The gun butt whacked the right side of my body so hard I nearly fell over.

"Brace it better," Dan said. "Like this." He showed me how.

I braced it against my shoulder, set my feet apart, and fired again. The sound of the gun resounded in my ear—in my brain—clearing out any lingering thoughts. The kick of the butt went through me from my shoulder to my chest like a shudder. After a while, I figured out a way to squint that almost worked, and then I could try to hit things—trees, branches. I liked it. Bang! Spewing bark and splintering green wood!

Firing into the gnarled, overgrown apple trees was a peculiar experience, but a powerful one. I could understand why guns fascinated some people. Power of any kind—real or artificially induced—was something I had not experienced in a long time.

One afternoon, when we were alone and likely to be so for hours, Dan and I sat on a wicker sofa on the long front porch of the house. I knew Dan would begin kissing me, and when he did I closed my eyes and acquiesced. Dan quickly maneuvered us into a horizontal position on the settee. My eyes opened—wide—and I was aware of my heart's alarmed, insistent beat. My hands began to perspire. I freed my mouth, but I didn't speak. Dan began to pull down my shorts. I kept my knees together.

"What are you *doing?*" I cried out. "Stop!"

Before, I had possessed something like desire, but no longer.

"How *can* you?" I asked him.

"Sorry," he said mildly, but with the confidence, it seemed to me, of one who was biding his time.

5

People confess only to previously concealed matters over which it is (or has been) possible, at least in principle, to exert some control, or for which they acknowledge at least shared responsibility.

Sissela Bok, *Secrets*

IN SEPTEMBER I entered my senior year in high school, and Dan left for the Midwest.

By now I had recovered just enough from my family's sadness and my own to begin to look around and appreciate the world again. My sister was doing remarkably well in college, and my mother was loving her library job. Life felt . . . possible. I began to be part of my school (as the Beach Boys sang), and I no longer felt that I was living down my past, pretending to be one person while feeling like another.

I applied to New England colleges, because Mrs. Maurice, my flamboyant tutor, had told me to. I was able to apply to good schools because my SAT scores were fairly high, as Mrs. Maurice had predicted they would be. The morning I took the tests I woke up feeling calm and sure; I remembered that this was going to be easy for me.

That fall, I began going to football games at school with new friends. The late evenings smelled of leafmold and damp earth. I loved Friday nights at the suburban playing field, where we packed ourselves warmly, tightly, into the bleachers and cheered our side. I loved having friends again, and I wrote to Dan about them. He wrote back angrily complaining that I had gone out on dates before he had given me permission to do so. In one letter, he says that he will agree to go to a Christmas dance with me at my high school if I promise not to parade him around. He reminds me that he doesn't like to meet people. He reminds me who is boss.

The letters veer between indignant recriminations and, on the other hand, beseeching requests for reassurance, followed by further insistence that Dan is the boss. I can remember feeling both frightened and repelled as I read them the first time. Now I read them as the poignant pleas of someone very young and inexperienced who is fighting a losing battle.

At one Friday night football game, I had noticed a boy talking with friends and laughing. When friends introduced us, we began to talk and couldn't seem to stop. It wasn't long before he asked me out. We were friends, but we held hands when we were together.

Richard DaVita's parents were New Yorkers, and while Richard hated the noise and grime of what is now my hometown, there was much about him—his open-mindedness, his humor, and his curiosity—that was entirely different from the insular world of Arlington. I gravitated to him for one of the reasons I eventually gravitated to New York: I could hold up my head, be myself, and belong.

When did I tell Richard about Dan and my pregnancy? I don't remember when, or what I said. I remember I cried, for form's sake. Lamentations of shame seemed only appropriate, but Richard said, "It could have happened to anyone. It just happened to you. God, I can't believe you've been through so much in your life."

In simultaneously recognizing my ordeal and dismissing the moral implications usually attached to it, Richard slowly rehabilitated me. Following his natural bent, Richard eventually became a psychotherapist. I have occasionally thought of myself as his first patient.

At Richard's house, his siblings, grandparents, and visiting Italian relatives were in and out, and we were all part of the flow of family life. I never wondered what the DaVitas would think if they knew about me. The secrecy of my situation seemed to work as it was meant to: I picked up the pieces of my life and got on with it.

I knew that getting on with it meant I had to break up with Dan. That fall, he invited me to his college for homecoming weekend.

It was cold and windy when I arrived. The leaves were beginning to drop from their branches. Remembering the brightly colored trees, I suppose I must have been there during daylight hours, but all I can recall, except for that bit of nature, is darkness.

Not long after I arrived, I sat next to Dan on the edge of a low sofa or bed, with my knees drawn up tensely in front of me. Dan did not believe me at first, when I told him that I was breaking up with him. Then he began to cry, and I was surprised. Somehow I had not quite known that he loved me, no matter what he said, perhaps because he was unable to make me feel loved. But I knew pain when I saw it, and this time it made me recoil in quick self-preservation. I could not afford to acknowledge the ache in his heart, because I would not be able to turn my back on him.

For some reason that even now I cannot quite fathom, my mother reacted with fevered rage at the news that I had broken up with Dan. We were driving back from a shopping center a few days after my trip when she began screaming at me in the car. I was ambushed, trapped, with no place to hide. I cringed as she railed against me, calling me a tramp and worse.

Was it possible that staying with Dan would actually have redeemed me in her eyes? Was that the proper punishment for me? Perhaps Mother was afraid that I would make the same mistake with a new boyfriend that I had made with the last. And it may have rankled her to see me rebounding from something that for her was probably still an open wound. She was a widow, with one daughter who was mentally ill and another who had given up an illegitimate child. I was the picture of resilient youth.

Staring out of the car window, trying not to hear my mother's horrible diatribe, I silently wrapped myself in thoughts of Richard's affectionate approbation and clung to the notion that I was a good person, one who deserved to live and to do so with some happiness.

The application form for Connecticut College for Women had many large, blank areas for long, written answers, and I took pains with it. Answering a question about what experience in my life had affected me most, I described the night my father died and how his death had changed everything, forever. I was accepted, but I had to fight with my mother to allow me to go, because I was also offered a scholarship to attend another school. Connecticut was expensive, she said. I *had* to go there, I countered recklessly. She gave in.

The summer after high school, I was hired as a temporary clerk-typist in the Interior Department's Bureau of Land Management. There was a redheaded secretary in the office who was seven or eight months pregnant. I watched her. She looked happy, completely unaware of the torment that awaited her. One day, in the ladies' room, she put a dime in the Kotex machine and turned the crank. Holding up the cardboard container as she marched to a stall, she said, "Bet you've never seen a pregnant woman use one of these, huh?" I laughed uncomfortably.

I almost never babysat, but I liked the neighbors—both musicians—in the house behind ours. When they asked if I would babysit one evening, I said yes. They had two young children whom I liked a lot, a boy and a girl, and that year they had a new baby, another girl.

The baby was sound asleep when I arrived. Before they went out the parents showed me how to warm and test her bottle.

After getting into his pajamas, the boy, then about six, asked me if I'd like to listen to music. Sure, I said. He began flipping confidently through a stack of LPs. "Do you like Tchaikovsky?" he asked, looking up. "He's *so* melodic." I laughed at his precocious taste and told him he'd have to show me. He picked *Romeo and Juliet*.

We listened together. "This is the sad part," he said at one point, as the music turned plangent.

After the symphony ended, the little boy and his sister kissed me goodnight, and I put them to bed.

Later the baby woke gently, with a whimper that gradually became a cry. I picked her up. Changed her diapers. Gave her a bottle, held her over my shoulder, listened attentively for the burp, jumped when it came—a resounding belch that squirted a trail of sour milk down my back—and then laughed at my own surprise. The baby smiled.

She was awake. What to do? I sang to her, and danced with her, and raised her over my head. Like her brother and sister, she was already a charming person. She didn't seem in the least suspicious of me, a comparative stranger. I took her ease at face value: She liked me. Eventually, she fell asleep in my arms and I put her back in her crib. Watching her sleep made my chest hurt. For much of the rest of the evening I held my hand over my heart.

I wondered if I could have mothered my own child. The sweet baby and her easygoing brother and sister made it hard not to think so. It was the first time I had considered that possibility. Of course this was only one short evening, but wasn't life just one evening after another?

When the parents returned, I walked home through the side yard. How was this night different from all other nights? It was the only time I had thought of the child I had relinquished as "my baby." It was the only moment when simple grief broke through my protective shell.

When the neighbors called me to babysit again, I made an excuse and said no.

In the fall, I left for college. There were many signs that I was not all right, but they may have seemed negligible compared with the Big Sign—my pregnancy—and that seemed to be over and done with. My grades, for instance, had been tumbling since adolescence but they were especially poor during my senior year. The last semester, I'd made a D in French. I had been a child for whom a B was unthinkable, in another life, before my sister's hospitalizations, and before my father's death, and before my pregnancy, and before the frightening birth, and before my mother gave up on me. At the beginning of junior high school, I was still an A student, but by the middle of high school I had become a girl whose ability to concentrate was nil, who got through classes by dint of some bit of verbal cleverness and the ability to write fairly well on short notice. I had become a glib, shallow student, and I was unable to admit to anyone that it was no longer possible for me to think or study.

My problem, if I understand it, was that I was expending an inordinate amount of intellectual energy maintaining my bright charade. It suited me, for I knew, as I had known instinctively when I returned to school after childbirth, that if I looked at my life I would have to pay some close attention to my father's death, to my sister's very rocky condition, to my pregnancy, and to the loss of my child. Loss, fear, shame, and more sorrow: the examined life was out of the question. That way led only to grief.

I have pictures of myself taken during my college years and I see a cheerful, happy face, but as a college student who wasn't stupid but could not cope, I found reason to doubt my sanity every day. I could not organize my time, read anything that required me to be analytical, or learn straight facts, such as dates. The sight of any number on the page of a textbook made me sweat. I would sit stiffly in my dorm room with a book of philosophy, reading the same paragraphs again and again and panicking that I couldn't hold a single thought in my head to the end of the page. I often cried.

Richard and I were at schools that were only a couple of hours apart, but I began to drift away from him: I had neither the imagination nor the stamina to wait through the intervals of our separations or be satisfied with weekend visits. I needed someone right where I could see him and touch him and make sure he was still there.

I felt crazy. I knew I wasn't exactly like my sister, but I was sure that if I relaxed my guard for a moment I might become even sicker than she was, and I might never recover. The cost of denying my pain was that whenever I accidentally caught an unwelcome glimpse of it it seemed immense, pervasive, fathomless.

Once, after setting aside a particularly absorbing novel that I had stayed up all night to finish, I could not figure out how to reenter the real world. After I set down the book I felt a whirling confusion and couldn't figure out what I was supposed to do next. I put myself in the college infirmary. After a day or two of doing nothing but lying in bed—no reading, no visitors—I had figured it all out again. Get up, eat breakfast, go to class or skip it, eat lunch, walk to the art studios, paint, eat supper, talk with friends, go to sleep. I checked out and went back to the dorm.

I was barely making it. I majored in art, where I could manage the encompassing, instinctual work of painting. But to get through other courses, I took diet pills, which nearly everyone seemed to have on hand. On amphetamines, I became calm and clear. If I took them while writing a paper, I received an A for a grade. I know now that children and teenagers with Attention Deficit Disorder are given stimulants, which paradoxically settle them down and make them able to concentrate. That was the effect diet pills had on me. They kept me awake, but not agitated. With amphetamines, I could calmly look at the page in my typewriter and quickly organize my thoughts for the next paragraph.

Probably today I would be treated with a combination of stimulants, antidepressants, and talk therapy—that is, if I put myself in treatment. At twenty, for me, the only thing worse than feeling crazy was admitting that I felt crazy.

One Friday night, my friend Ruth smoked a joint at a mixer. I was in the dorm, smoking Larks and reading Donne, weeping with him for a broken heart that after one such love could love no more, when I heard Ruth's door slam at the end of the hall. I went and listened, but heard nothing inside. I tapped.

"Go away."

I went in. Ruth was rocking on her bed, clinging to her knees. It was a crisis—I could see that—and crises were familiar to me. I could not handle a date on the page of a history textbook, but a crisis was a different story.

"What did you do?" I asked.

"A joint. A big one."

"You're going straight to the infirmary," I said. I wrapped Ruth in a blanket and walked her over.

In a day or two, Ruth's parents came to take her away to McLean, a private psychiatric hospital near Boston. The episode with the marijuana or hashish, or whatever it had been, was only the catalyst for a breakdown that had been incipient for weeks. Ruth wanted to go to McLean; she felt out of control, constantly anxious, and worried that she was going mad.

I felt that way too. Was that any reason to break step?

Ruth asked me if I would visit her. One Saturday a month later, I took a bus to Boston and then another to McLean. I was taken upstairs to Ruth's ward. After I was let in, the door was shut behind me and I heard a key turn in the lock. As Ruth and I walked the halls, I was comforted by the simple fact that I passed for well. Ruth talked nervously but freely, expressing all her self-doubts and giving short shrift to her own intelligence and good sense. I, pacing the halls with her in my emperor's new cloak of confidence, did the opposite. If I didn't watch my step, I thought, someone would see that I was finally on the right side of the door to the cuckoo's nest.

6

---

*It is harder to hide feelings
we have than to feign those
we lack.*

La Rochefoucauld

THE SUMMER AFTER my sophomore year I began doing a long
stretch of time in which various men, usually ones I worked
with, stood in for the love of my life, whoever he would be. I
embarked on a feverish search, frantic to find the one who would
make me a married woman, and, more important, a mother—a real
one, legitimizing me to the world and, most of all, to myself. Make
an honest woman of me.

I was less depressed than I had been during the years immediately
following my father's death and my pregnancy, but my mind was
hardly healthy. There was a great wall the size of China's separating
my focus from my inner self, which would remain terra incognita for
at least another decade. Although I kept busy, I was just marking
time until I could find someone suitable.

I needed a savior. I met men everywhere—at school, at the government office where I worked, in the neighborhood—and I offered
tryouts to a wide field, but most of the ones I sampled were disappointing. For starters, they were too young—in other words, no
older than I was. Few were fatherlike, and the ones that were had
children already. And wives. I zinged in and out of love affairs,
looking for a future where I could stay put.

My nights were plagued by a recurrent nightmare, in which a

darkening net gradually enclosed me, shutting out light and air and eventually suffocating me. The same dream had tormented me as a child, when I had woken up screaming. As a near-adult, I didn't scream, but when I woke up sweating, with a pounding heart, I would lie in the dark and wonder if I had finally crossed over. Despite my ability to function, I knew my state of mind was dangerously chaotic.

"I need to see someone," I told my mother.

"Who?"

"A psychiatrist," I said.

"Why?"

"I need to. I really do." I was firm and clear, and, as usual at such times, my mother paid attention. I called McLean, and someone referred me to a doctor in the Washington area. I made an appointment.

The doctor was a young man with a kind face. Much of our talk at the first appointment centered around my mother, and at one point he suggested that her sense of "personal boundaries" was faulty. Ah, my poor mother: She had been blamed for my sister's schizophrenia and now she got sandbagged again for whatever was wrong with me.

True to the doctor's prediction, that evening my mother asked what had happened at the appointment. Against his advice, I went ahead and told her, knowing that it might make her uncomfortable but at the same time reasoning that it might open some sort of dialogue that would lead to a new and better relationship for us.

At ten o'clock, Mother dialed the doctor's number and then stuck the receiver in my hand, so that I could tell him I would not be returning to therapy. "There's no way in hell you can make me pay for that crap!" was, I believe, how she put it.

Life continued to be fraught with disjunction. By the end of sophomore year, as I had become accustomed to college life, I had made the dean's list. In spite of that, I impulsively transferred to the

University of Colorado because a boy who had broken up with me was still in Connecticut and I couldn't bear to be where I might run into him.

A few weeks after arriving in Boulder for my junior year, I began seeing a man who was studying for his doctorate in anthropology. One night he mentioned a fellow graduate student, a woman in his department. "She needs a job to support herself," he said. "She's a mother."

"I'm a mother, too," I answered absent-mindedly.

He waited.

Embarrassed, I explained. It felt good to tell, but not for long.

My new friend listened impassively. Then he clarified his remark. "I mean a *real* mother."

The following summer I went home to Virginia, as always, but this time, I went there with the intention of staying, for although home was the last place I wanted to be it was also the only one in which I felt free to hole up. It was a sick place; I was a sick girl. For once it felt right, if not exactly good, to be there. I decided to take a year off from school.

The office where I worked hired me as a full-time clerk-typist. To become a regular civil-service appointee, I had to take a government test. I scored 99 on it, and the secretary who was my boss smiled approvingly.

"Just like Ivory," she said.

Ninety-nine percent pure. That was me.

After a year of the comforts of workaday work and bimonthly checks, I returned to Connecticut.

I was better. It was six years since the death of my father; five since the birth of my baby. The past would always trouble me, but at least it had become the slightly distant past.

When I'd started college, I had blithely engaged in various forms of dangerous behavior—hitchhiking alone, for instance—that, while perhaps mild by today's standards of bad judgment and self-destruction, were indicative of the low esteem in which I held life in general and mine in particular. But now, at twenty-two, I set about my days in a more or less orderly way. I never skipped a class. I did my homework to the extent that I could. I went to bed every night and got up every morning. I worked at painting as regularly as I had worked at my clerk's job, but for longer hours. I settled into a relatively peaceful, loveless life. My only worry was what I would do after graduation.

The answer appeared in the cafeteria of my dorm one evening in late October. I noticed a boy I'd met some years back. George stayed that night in my room, and within a few months we had decided to get married. Spurning the women's movement, I would say to my friends, "I just want to be his wife. I'll follow him wherever he decides to go." As a sentimental girl group had sung, there wasn't an ocean too deep, a mountain so high it could keep, *keep* me away! Ruth, who was fresh out of McLean, a physics honors student on her way to graduate school, now says she used to "just about puke" listening to me.

It was 1971, when many people we knew were deciding to live together instead of marrying, but I was nothing if not traditional. George and I married the day after graduation.

I've often said that my young husband and I chose the University of Washington after seeing the movie *Five Easy Pieces* and falling in love with the Northwest landscape, but I think it was really because George was offered several financial inducements to study mathematics there, and those tipped the scale when we were deciding on graduate schools. There was also a large art department, where I could go for a masters degree. George's grandparents gave us a wintergreen 1960 Rambler that looked like an overturned bathtub and needed sheet metal bolted to its rusty fenders in order to pass inspection. In late August, we took off for the Northwest, camping across the country, carrying all our possessions, including two ten-speed bikes, in or on top of the car.

In some ways we were very happy together, both of us casual and fond of the outdoors. But I had probably married for the same reason I'd left Richard: I needed someone literally by my side in order to go forward with life. I could not be alone, and I knew it. It turned out that I chose well. My husband was not only loyal, but also easygoing in a way that allowed me wide scope to explore my abilities and interests. He knew all about my having given up a child, but it seemed unimportant to him. Where Richard had had a clear sense of my suffering, my young husband shrugged it off. It was in the past, I hardly talked about it, and it didn't matter to him.

It mattered to me, whether I knew it or not, and I feel now that I duped George as I duped myself. Inside my shiny shell, I was vulnerable to every grain of doubt and dissatisfaction, especially where close relationships with men were concerned. We began graduate school, we had an active social life with many friends, and yet I could not relax. My marriage was all I thought about, but I couldn't get it right. I fought with my husband about everything, testing his loyalty at every turn.

Once again I became deeply troubled. Finally I went to the university clinic and made an appointment with the school psychologist. The therapy she provided was excellent, but I used it poorly. I went to her office each week for a tune-up, as it were, when what I needed was a rebuilt engine. I never told her about my pregnancy. It wasn't until the final appointment that I told her about my sister's mental illness—the great secret in my life. Luckily that was enough for the hour; I didn't have to mention the other. I was done with my master's degree; I was no longer eligible for her services. She referred me to a private psychiatrist, but I did not go. I had looked for help because I had been suicidal again; having patched myself up, I decided I was done.

Although as always I loved and longed for children, watching babies in strollers and toddlers in parks as raptly then as I do now, I abruptly left my marriage as I would continue to abandon every one of my serious relationships until I was nearly forty. The simple truth was that without confronting my memories I could not become fully formed. I needed to shed skin after skin, year after year, until I became myself—a person whom I wouldn't meet for a long time to come. With my young husband, a man who was patient and truehearted, I was able to decompensate, as psychiatric jargon describes it: I took advantage of the safe asylum of his companionship to fall apart, at least to a degree, and to experience some of the sadness that had been hidden inside me for years. The sadness was so extreme, however, that I was reluctant to delve deeper, to its source.

I could not do what I most longed to do: have a family. It has taken me thirty years to wonder if perhaps the ordeals I had suffered made it impossible for me to regard pregnancy or family life with equanimity. I wanted a baby, this I knew, but in my heart I could not trust a man. Testing and testing and testing George's patience was the only way I could try to prove to myself that he would not leave me when I needed him most. Testing him was ultimately not enough for me. Nothing could make me certain that a man would stay. The only thing I could do to protect myself was to make sure that I left first. That way, I would not expose myself to the possibility of another abandonment.

It wasn't just Dan's "abandonment." It wasn't even primarily that, I think. It was my father's. In dying, he had left me. Even now I notice that when I love my second husband beyond measure I instantly step back a bit and even occasionally have a flashback of my father dying. At least it's right there where I can see it: I am afraid of losing any man I love. Nothing could be simpler, once I figured it out. But with my first husband the past was still too close to see clearly.

A few years after our divorce I moved back East, to New York. My life was in disorder, as usual, which seemed to suit me, where stability apparently did not. I could begin and begin and begin again, but I could not last. The continual changes I required took many forms—new apartments, new painting studios, new men. That time, that year—1979—the alterations I made were monumental. I moved across country, I stopped painting, and I sank into a perfectly destructive affair with a married man. He was much older than I was and deeply committed to his marriage, if not to fidelity. He also had an adopted child, whom he adored.

This all dovetailed nicely with my neurotic interests: I could tell myself that I was not starting a family because of course it was impossible with him—he already had one (two, actually, counting offspring from an earlier marriage). And because he was already with someone else I didn't worry that he would leave me: he was already gone, as it were. What I found most thrilling, though, was observing his tender, thoughtful, sensitive concern for his adopted child. I ached when his son had a problem; I breathed easily again when it was solved. I felt like the boy's spying birth mother, and I was satisfied with the love this son received from his father, who was otherwise breathtakingly self-absorbed.

I often practiced only rather slapdash birth control, and I never became pregnant. I had had a uterine infection, and though it never developed into pelvic inflammatory disease, I knew that there might be some permanent damage to my fallopian tubes. And in my late twenties I'd had a Pap test that showed pre-cancerous cells. Cryocautery removed them, but cryocautery was also known to inhibit fertility. In addition to the possible physical reasons for my lack of fertility, I believe that my subconscious fears were the best birth-control I could have had. These were manifold: if I love a man, he will die (my father); if I have a child, that child will be mentally ill (my sister); if I become pregnant, I will lose the baby (as I had lost the first).

I was now thirty-one, and I had spent a decade and a half keeping such fears as far from my thoughts as possible, as much of the time as I could. But as I closed, one by one, the doors to all the rooms that frightened me, my depression became nearly debilitating. One winter night, coming home from work on a bus, I looked out the window into the well-lit streets of Manhattan and could not focus my eyes. I made it to my apartment, unlocked the door, and went inside. Without turning on the light, I doubled over, physically ill with depression. I could not go on, not even into another room.

The next day, I began therapy, ostensibly to try to resolve my feelings about the adoptive father-figure, the married man—the perfect one through whom to deconstruct my psyche. I knew that I needed help to put this philanderer, and the complex of neuroses that fueled my love for him, behind me. That was enough to start on.

PART THREE

Second Chances

7

You could take one look at the sky and know it was the perfect time of night for a miracle.

Alice Hoffman, *Fortune's Daughter*

FOR THE FIRST YEAR, I cried. If my psychiatrist had placed a Kleenex surcharge on my bill each month, I would have accepted the fairness of her gesture. One morning, I wept as I confessed, "I can't seem to get along without a man."

"Why should you?" she asked.

The question caught me up short, but after only a moment of reflection I knew the answer: Because a man can disappear. Just like *that*. For eight years of weekly sessions I tracked that grief through layer upon layer of memory and experience.

At thirty-one, I stumbled into a job at a news magazine, answering letters to the editor. I needed work, and I was in doubt about my ability to go on painting. I had run out of whatever it took to spend long hours alone in my studio. Working at the magazine, I was in the company of smart, funny, and talented people. The job forced me to focus beyond my own life. Although it was wrenching to stop painting I knew that where daily work was concerned I needed to live at a shallower level. It was warmer in the shallows.

Year by year, my life improved. My general vagueness lifted, and I eventually forgot how it felt to want out of this wonderful life. I realized with surprise that I was happy alone. I was able to concentrate, write, and make plans.

Then, as these things sometimes happen, I met a man, an artist, who was so obviously meant to be mine that neither pursuit nor resistance was imaginable. We would be together, and that was that. We met at a dinner party, where we bickered mildly over something small but irritating. The next day, when one of the guests called our hosts to thank them, he asked, "How long have Peggy and Harvey been married?" We didn't hear about the comment until many months later, when we finally went out for the first time.

We both were busy; we almost forgot about each other. I remember feeling that it didn't matter: There was no way to evade my future with this person whom I saw only occasionally, accidentally, and in passing. I wasn't sure when that future would begin, but I could wait.

Two months after I met Harvey, my mother died suddenly of a stroke. In shock, I took care of her funeral and began in a haphazard way to settle her estate, but my primary concern was to try to see that my sister's life remained stable. I eventually heard about a group, the National Alliance for the Mentally Ill, which offered a siblings' meeting in New York. When I went to these meetings, I found to my relief that the other siblings there had many of the same worries that had paralyzed me many times, including the fear of having children who might become mentally ill. The meetings became my greatest comfort, as I began to be able to see my sister's problems for what they were: the fallout of a debilitating illness. Gradually, I focused more on the illness than on Sally's particular quirks, and finally our relationship, over a long period of time and through some harrowing crises, improved greatly.

I had always known about the genetic component of mental illness. Even as a child I knew. My great aunt had spent more than a decade of her long life in a mental hospital. My great uncle had been indisputably manic-depressive, and my mother had suffered a period of postpartum psychosis for which she had been hospitalized for more than half a year. It seemed to me that there was a strong chance some damaged genes might have polluted the pool that produced me, and it wasn't until years of therapy had improved my judgment and engendered some confidence in my own sanity that I really believed I would not become sick like Sally. Never did I consciously wonder if my son was mentally ill, however. I would be tidying up the end of this book before I realized how much, and for how long, that fear had pressed on my mind. The one for whom I worried was always my *possible* child—the one I could keep. The one I no longer expected to have.

Harvey and I eventually got together, and when we did it was as I had known it would be. I thought I had decided, finally, that I was not unhappy with the thought of remaining childless. I was forty, and I felt old. I was exhausted with caring for my sister and settling my mother's estate, and I was also comfortable with Harvey and happy to be going out, traveling some, and seeing friends together. When I first met him, I had talked to the friend who introduced us about the possibility of having a child. During that dreamy conversation, I was suffused with hope. But when I returned to life as I was actually living it at the time—frequent trips to Virginia, late hours working, constant worry about Sally—I completely forgot my deepest desires.

Then in the fall of 1988, our AMI sibling group invited a geneticist to speak at one of our meetings about hereditary aspects of mental illness. She gave a fascinating talk about a family she had studied, pointing to diagrams and charts showing the progression of schizophrenia down through several generations. At the end of her lecture, someone asked what the likelihood would be of our passing on the disease to our children. "The chances of the well sibling of a schizophrenic person having a child with schizophrenia are about the same as the normal population," she said, "give or take a percentage point." It was not schizophrenia that ran in my family, but my heart leapt at the statistic. I remember nearly dancing downtown to Harvey's place at the end of the lecture.

Despite my general distractedness, my reproductive system was experiencing an irresistible combination of circumstances: my mother's death (and my seemingly innate desire to replace a life with a life, as I had after my father died); the geneticist's assurances; and my own realization that for me time was running out.

December, I missed a period. That had happened before.

Early January. I felt a bit ill, but mostly in the evenings. And it was an odd sort of ill: Dorito chips and salsa appealed to me; plain food turned my stomach. I chalked it up to worry, and to late nights and holiday celebrations. Six months before, I'd missed a period, but then everything had gone along more or less as before. My gynecologist told me to expect such changes after age thirty-five. So this time I figured these disturbances were just a precursor to menopause.

After two months, though, I decided to use a home pregnancy test. When, the next morning, I saw the stick turn pink, my reaction was immediate: My eyes looked up and I whispered, "Thank You."

As I walked the three or four steps from the bathroom to my bedroom, I felt a sensation I'd felt only once before (the first time I saw Paris): it was as if my feet were not touching the ground. I was floating—that old cliché. I smiled as I levitated abstractedly past a foolish face in the mirror on my closet door. I would have to do something about that face before getting on the subway and going to work.

That night I told Harvey. I watched his expression carefully. I wanted to try to gauge his spontaneous reaction to this momentous news, not wait for whatever words he might find appropriate to use. Although his murmured words were, "I'm not sure I want another child" (he was in his fifties and the father of a grown daughter), his face said, I am filled with wonder and joy.

8

Within minutes after my son was born, I felt as if I had regained full use of my heart.

Jan Waldron, *Giving Away Simone*

IN DECEMBER, I flew to Pittsburgh to spend Christmas with my cousin, her husband, their two children, and my sister. On the way back I was sick with nausea and diarrhea, and before long I was dehydrated and weak. Suddenly my evening queasiness disappeared. My breasts stopped hurting. I didn't feel pregnant.

I went to my obstetrician, Dr. Chin, an old friend whom I called by her first name, Jeannie, who looked more concerned than I'd expected. "There's very little chance we can pick up a heartbeat yet," she said. "So do *not* panic when we can't. It probably means nothing. We'll just have to wait." She affixed a listening device to my abdomen and set up her stethoscope. She listened. Her face relaxed. And then, without a word, she slipped the stethoscope into my ears. Da*dup* da*dup* da*dup* da*dup*.

I had signed a contract to write a book about my sister's illness and how it had affected our family, and so I took a leave of absence from my job in order to write full-time. What I did, instead, was sit. I sat on the frayed, old loveseat in my quiet apartment and watched reruns of "Cannon," "Barnaby Jones," and "Hawaii 5-O." I sat on the loveseat reading and re-reading *What to Expect When You're Expecting*. I did nothing, really, but gestate. I sat on the loveseat and felt the fetus kick. I talked and cooed to it. I patted my stomach when the fetus had hiccups. I sang to it. I received an inheritance from my favorite aunt, and I spent it on time. I took that time and used it well—making, making, making the baby. I sat on the loveseat and decided I did not want to write about my sister's mental illness while I was pregnant. Too many painful memories—who knew how it could affect a fetus? I was completely in love with this baby.

I never once felt free to love my son as he grew inside of me. Not only did I avoid thinking of him as a baby, I rarely thought of myself as pregnant. In ignoring my condition, I had floated in my bubble of denial, waiting until I could resume my "real" life—the fine one, the fake one. Thinking of that little fetus surrounded for the first few months by intense anxiety, my one comfort is that at Mrs. Blake's I had relaxed. At least that much of my son's prenatal life took place in a womb that was well-nourished, rested, and, most days, peaceful.

During my late, miracle pregnancy, I called the doctor's office every week or so with some new crisis—some little twinge or other that I was sure signalled danger. I had shooting pains in my upper thighs—stretching ligaments, I was told—and pains in my lower abdomen—stretching muscles. My cousin was coming to visit; one of her children had been exposed to chicken pox. Thanksgiving had occurred during the first week of my pregnancy, when I'd had no symptoms, and I'd drunk two-and-a-half glasses of red wine that day. Later I'd read *The Broken Cord,* Michael Dorris's book on fetal alcohol syndrome, which warns readers of the importance of complete abstinence from alcohol during the earliest stages of embryonic development. Dr. Chin or her nurse, Linda, spoke to me always in the sort of calming, stroking voice one reserves for upset children or sick animals.

At the beginning, Harvey was slow to accommodate the idea of becoming a father again. I talked it over with Dr. Chin, and she told me to bring him to my next appointment. After the pelvic, she called him into the examining room. She set up the stethoscope to listen to the baby's heartbeat, saying to him as she worked, "This will blow you away."

"Nothing blows him away," I said, watching Harvey's determinedly placid expression.

"This will," said Jeannie. At that, the look on Harvey's face turned from neutral to negative.

She hooked the stethoscope into his ears.

I will never forget the sudden, startled, beatified, believing yet unbelieving look on his face. Jeannie and I burst out laughing.

"Shh!" he hissed.

After that, he called the baby "Thumper."

Throughout the pregnancy, my doctor knew, as well as she could, that everything was fine. "There's always one like you to drive us crazy," Jeannie said to me later—much later—but she and Linda kindly took the trouble to feign concern whenever I called. I asked them if they had ever worried. "Why?" Linda asked, sincerely puzzled. The doctor did only one ultrasound, with the amniocentesis, and otherwise left it to nature to take its course without undue scrutiny. I, on the other hand, waited every morning for the baby's first kick of the day.

I was sure I would lose this child.

I couldn't get to the bottom of that anxiety. I suspect now that my fear had something to do with buried guilt for having given up my first child—some subconscious conviction that I would be punished for that by losing this one—but I can't say for certain. I didn't think about the long-ago pregnancy; I wanted my joy in the new one to eclipse my memories of the first. I didn't want to remember it, and anyway it was far in the past. And yet the past kept nagging me, subconsciously reminding me of my old loss—the loss of what should be the raison d'être of any pregnancy, the baby.

In a fever of worry, I almost skipped the amniocentesis, weighing the risks of miscarriage against those of Down Syndrome, which were almost equal, for a mother of my age. Finally, I reasoned that in New York City, in Mount Sinai Hospital, with a gifted obstetrician performing the amnio, my chances of miscarriage from the test were probably far lower than the national average. I decided it was irresponsible to refuse. I cared about mental retardation. That was the only condition, I decided, that would tempt me to abort this fetus—severe retardation. Harvey and I were not young. "I don't care if it has arms and legs," I told the doctor firmly. "Just so it can compose an angry letter demanding equal rights." I wanted this soul in whatever form God saw fit to bestow upon it.

The hospital doctor watching the sonogram screen during the amnio smiled and murmured, "Your baby looks beautiful." Two and a half weeks later, we received the news that the amnio was clear.

"Do you want to know the baby's sex?" the woman on the telephone asked me.

"It's a girl," I said. "I just know."

"You're right." she said.

For months I forgot my previous pregnancy, except when I marveled that this time I had no fainting spells. But then I began to show. Soon I learned simply to say "Yes" when anyone asked the inevitable question: "Is this your first?"

And an hour later, "Is this your first?"

Yes. In important ways, yes.

I finally became desensitized to the question.

Then one morning toward the end of my pregnancy, I woke up terrified. I had a doctor's appointment that day. As soon as I was seated on the examining table, I blurted, "Jeannie, I'm really, really scared. I don't think I'm going to be all right."

"What are you afraid of?" she asked.

"The pain." She had mentioned that because of the time interval—nearly a quarter of a century, as the amnio interviewer had so jauntily put it—this birth would probably be much like a first delivery, rather than a second. The first, as I suddenly remembered it, was something I didn't want to go through again. I told Jeannie I was stiff with fear every time I thought of it.

As always, she was reassuring. "You'll do fine. And don't worry, there will be a nurse to coach you. Harvey will be there. This time'll be different."

I shook my head.

She took my hand. "You won't be alone."

On August 17, 1989 I was having lunch with my friend Nancy at Wolf's Deli, an enormous, popular restaurant at the busy intersection

of West Fifty-seventh Street and Sixth Avenue, when my water
broke. I had read somewhere that the baby's head rests in the pelvic
cavity and effectively stoppers the drain, as it were, allowing only a
trickle of amniotic fluid to leak out, and so I was unprepared for
the smaller version of Niagara Falls that gushed from beneath my
maternity dress and cascaded in torrents from the seat of our booth
to the floor of the restaurant, where it ran in rivulets around our
sandaled feet.

Waitresses quickly came with mops and towels and whisked me
to the women's room, where I could see that the amniotic fluid was
stained a faintly greenish color. That, I knew, meant that there was a
substance called meconium in it. Meconium can signal fetal distress.

"I think I'm supposed to go straight to the hospital if there's
meconium," I told Nancy, who was busy squeezing the hem of my
dress between dry towels. She rushed to the street and hailed a taxi.

Later that afternoon, in the hospital, I was given pitocin, a drug
that speeds labor. "We'll try to mimic a normal birth, more or less,"
the doctor said. She predicted I would be in labor another eight
hours, so she made plans to go out for a bite to eat.

The contractions began to come one on top of another, without
pause. I was frightened, as I'd suspected I would be. I couldn't
breathe, or count, or look at the clock.

Most of the women I know have been astonished by childbirth,
and I was, too. But for me, so afraid of something going wrong, the
pain was like a distress flare. I was sure this could not possibly be
normal, even while I knew that it probably was. My labor nurse was
bored and tired. Harvey was holding my hand encouragingly. I
could see that I was the only one in the room who was coming
unglued. I asked for an epidural. When it took effect, I finally began
to relax.

Almost immediately, I felt an urge to push.

"It's too soon," the nurse said.

"Well, I . . . I really feel it," I ventured.

Desultorily, she pulled on sterile gloves and checked.

"Dr. Chin!" she shouted, without removing her hand.

Ten minutes later, my beautiful daughter was born.

Laura's umbilical cord had been wrapped around her neck (to this day she will not tolerate a scarf), and she had indeed been in distress at times, but she was plump and apparently healthy. Her lungs had to be suctioned because of the meconium, and so she was placed on a table a few feet from me, where nurses were waiting. They put her under a strong light and she jerked her head away (not blind); someone dropped a pan and she jumped (not deaf); they stuck a syringe down her throat and she bellowed (not mute); and finally, finally, they handed her to me. Immediately, she stopped crying and went to sleep.

Soon, they took her away to the nursery, while I was placed first in a recovery room and then, late that night, on the maternity ward.

I *had* to have my baby with me. I pressed the call bell, but no one came. Our first separation, those few hours, was the hardest I have yet endured. I couldn't shake the feeling that I might not see her again. I had already had more of her than I ever had of my son: I had seen her, I had held her. She was real, I knew, but I needed to see her again to make sure, and to make sure that I would not lose her here at the hospital, where, if my experience had taught me anything, I knew that babies could disappear.

Nurses came and went outside my door. There was a small baby boom in 1989, and my daughter was among a group whose arrivals form a peak in the chart that summer. The hospital was crammed with mothers; it was impossible to get anyone's attention. Finally I just got up, walked to the nursery, and demanded my child.

The supervisor in the newborn nursery did not respond to the urgency in my voice. She slowly checked and then re-checked the strip of plastic fastened around my wrist, making sure its numbers matched those on Laura's tiny ankle bracelet. (Good! I thought. They're *careful*.)

"Is this your first?" I was asked—that question, again—and I didn't know what to say. It seemed important not to lie to a nurse, after all. And in fact I felt no shame, just confusion as to why they wanted to know. "No," I answered truthfully. Laura was put in my arms. The nurses, assuming I had another child at home, didn't bother to show me what to do—how to nurse her or hold her or change her or bathe her. As it happened, I didn't need the nurses, but it would be a couple of years before I figured out why I had been left to my own devices, when my friends in other hospitals had been hovered over and instructed.

"Bring her back after you've nursed her," the nurse said.

"Mmm," I answered, with calculated imprecision.

I carried my miracle down the hall, climbed into bed, raised the metal bars on either side, nursed her, and slept on and off through the night with her on my chest—waking often in a great dream of peace to look at her and to feel her roundness, her reality, through the thin blanket. She seemed sweetly happy. My own happiness was something approaching a state of grace.

The next morning, a nurse chastised me. "You forgot to take her back to the nursery," she said.

"Mmm."

"Tonight? Call a nurse if you're too tired."

"Mmmm."

We spent the next night together, of course, and we all went home the following day, Harvey carrying Laura. As we left the hospital, I almost glanced back over my shoulder, my guilty relief augmented by the distant memory of my young self, leaving a maternity ward with my mother, instead of my child.

I worried that I might feel like a thief. Happily, I did not. This baby, like the first, was mine, but this one was mine to keep.

The day we brought Laura home, she slept on Harvey's shoulder for more than four hours without stirring. We were afraid to put her down, for fear of jostling her out of her newborn slumber. After an hour, I went to the corner grocery for milk, juice, and bread. It was odd to be alone for the first time in nine months.

When I was fifteen I had avoided thinking of the fetus within me as a child, a baby, a person. I'd ignored his kicking as I had ignored my own body. With Laura, it was the opposite. She was real to me from the moment the white plastic stick turned pink. After I found out she was a girl I spoke to her always as my daughter. I loved her whole-heartedly as she grew inside me, and I felt I knew her. For one thing she seemed considerate, if it does not seem too odd to say such a thing. She was wrong-way-up at one point, and because there is a higher rate of mental illness among breach babies, or so I had read in the *New York Times,* and because my sister was breach, I asked Laura to right herself. Within a week, her head turned down into my pelvic cavity. Thank you, I would say, whispering toward my belly. I appreciate that, Sweet Darling.

I had been concerned about two things while I was pregnant: one, that I would lose this pregnancy; two, that my child would be an uneasy baby, one whose psyche I would fret about endlessly, looking for signs that she was like my sister, inconsolable from birth. As if to dispel my fears, Laura was born on time and born healthy. Before long I was able to see that she was indeed the reasonable person I'd anticipated. I, however, was a basket case, leaping to her side at the slightest whimper, wanting to ensure that her tiny life was as stress-free as I could make it, because I knew that stress could contribute to the onset of mental illness. My sister's problems had begun in childhood: I would see to it that if Laura was going to develop mental illness it would not be exacerbated by any discomfort that I could allay.

Laura seemed fine. She was a baby with whom one could discuss and explain things. I liked to call her the Henry Clay of babies, after the Great Compromiser. When she was only six months old, crying at being taken from a swing in the park and put into her stroller to go home, she would calm instantly when I explained to her that it was time for lunch, and then nap, and that later, if it stayed sunny, we could come back.

Laura still responds gracefully to reason—most of the time. She's an enthusiast. She's funny, earnest, and kind. She is easy to love. Was my son easy to love? Did his parents decide to adopt a second child because their first, my first, was, like Laura, also a delight? The happiness Laura has brought to us is a gift for which Harvey and I never stop thanking God and each other.

Unlike some birth mothers I have met, I was unaware of thoughts about my first child for a long, long time. It didn't seem particularly odd to me that except for the first trip to the grocery I did not spend a single minute away from Laura until she was nearly six months old. It was easy to take her along to dinners and parties, because her disposition was usually pleasing and her habits fairly regular. It didn't seem strange to me that the first time I left her alone with a babysitter I broke out in hives at the hairdresser, or ran from the subway station to the apartment. It didn't seem strange to me that when I finally allowed a babysitter to take Laura to the park one day and they were two minutes late returning, I began to sweat as I watched the time tick by. I met them at the door with ashen skin and a questioning look.

Babysitters can be marvelously adaptive, and mine, or rather Laura's, learned to save an extra half-hour to meet and greet Laura's friendly neighbors on our city block, who would stop her and ask about Laura's progress and take Laura's pretty face in their hands and cry, "Oh, mi muñequita." The babysitter learned to risk being early—the relieved and delighted look on the mother's face—rather than take the chance of being even a moment late.

Working at home on my first book meant that until Laura was nine or ten months old, the babysitter could entertain her on the rug behind me as I sat at my word processor. I hired the babysitter for seven hours a day, but I still nursed Laura every two or three hours, ate lunch with her, checked her wraps before she went out, and welcomed her home again. I made sure I finished the first draft of my book before Laura could walk.

After the book was done, I employed the babysitter only occasionally. I couldn't bear to be away from Laura for long stretches—and a couple of hours seemed like a long stretch. At two, Laura began to object to separating from me at all and refused to leave the house when a sitter came to take her out to the playground. Instead of helping us all pass this typical developmental milestone, I let the babysitter go. For a year or more I wrote during naptime or not at all.

It was not until Laura was three and I enrolled her in a five-morning-a-week preschool class at the YMCA that I had to face what were clearly my own separation problems. I expected her to cling to me, and she did. I expected to have a hard time taking the little steps that would lead to real separation—sitting in the hall for a while, going out for coffee—and I did. What I did not expect was that after a couple of weeks, when Laura was adjusted and I was congratulating myself on how really well it had all gone, I would begin to feel sick— heartsick, soulsick, headsick—and get through each three-hour morning absence only by dint of enormous effort. I would check my watch for the twentieth time, leave home too early to pick her up, and watch through a face-size window in the door of her classroom until it was time for the teachers to open it.

I began to laugh about it—"School? Oh, Laura's fine, but I need to go back into therapy to deal with separation." It was another joke—good laughs—but of course it wasn't really a joke at all.

9

She stood apart from moral interests, yet close beside them, like a ghost that revisits the familiar fireside, and can no longer make itself seen or felt; no more smile with the household joy, nor mourn with the kindred sorrow; or, should it succeed in manifesting its forbidden sympathy, awakening only terror and repugnance. These emotions, in fact, and its bitterest scorn besides, seemed to be the sole portion that she retained in the universal heart.

Nathaniel Hawthorne, *The Scarlet Letter*

WHY WAS I SO slow to catch on?

On Easter Sunday 1992, while Laura and her friend Patrick were painting eggs and each other in our living room, Patrick's mother, Michelle, a successful, prolific writer, followed me into the kitchen for paper towels. She had just read my book about Sally and me, and she praised me lavishly. After giving me thirty seconds or so to bask in the warmth of her glowing review, she said, "So what are you working on now? What's next?"

"Jesus, Shelly, I don't know. I'm not even thinking about it."

"Well, what *I'm* dying to read is the story of what it was like to be fifteen and pregnant in 1965. I mean, 1965 was bad enough without *that*."

"Ugh," I said, or something to that effect, as I flung myself against the counter and pretended to pull a knife from my gut.

"Eviscerating, perhaps," Michelle said brightly, "but oh-so-cathartic!"

I thought about it from a purely pragmatic point of view, as if I were in consultation with a career counselor. Well, yes; that would make an interesting story. Too bad it wasn't someone *else's* story, though.

"I want to be a biographer," I said vaguely. "Dig up *unfamiliar* skeletons."

"Suit yourself," Michelle sang as she left with the towels, "but I really think personal pain is your forte."

I had to admit, if only to myself, that various memories were bothering me, most noticeably whenever I joked about separating from Laura. I was beginning, just barely, to put two and two together, and it finally dawned on me that I was *frightened* when Laura was out of my sight. Other parents might think occasionally about the possibility of their child being taken from them—but I was afraid of it every time I took Laura outside. My eyes were on her from the moment we left until we returned to the house, from sidewalk to sandbox to swings.

About the time Michelle made her suggestion, I was beginning to see that, in my semi-conscious, unexamined reasoning, "strangers" had "taken" a child of mine once before. Had I thought that consciously, even for a second, at sixteen? I don't believe so. I don't think I had a clue to my real emotions about losing my first baby until I began to guard my second with the vigilance of a nesting bird who has merely heard a twig snap in a nearby woods.

All of a sudden there seemed to be articles on adoption in every magazine and newspaper I picked up. That spring I read a long piece about a prospective adoptive couple and the pregnant woman, a college student, for whom they were caring and whose baby they would adopt at birth. The adoptive parents appeared to accept at face value the assurances of the birth mother that she was longing to help them make a family and that she felt as if she had been chosen to bring a child to them. I knew that her blithe certainty was completely false. And yet while I could see through her—in the end she did break down, though she went through with the decision to give up her child—I could not see into myself.

Almost a year later, in March 1993, I opened a copy of *The New Yorker* and noticed a piece called "The War for Baby Clausen." The subhead said, "A bitter two-year custody battle over a baby girl has challenged the law—and become a cause célèbre for anti-adoption activists." The piece chronicled the DeBoer-Schmidt case in the Midwest, which I mentioned at the beginning of this book, in which a prospective adoptive couple, Robbie and Jan DeBoer, were fighting a court order to return a child they called Jessica to her biological parents, Cara and Dan Schmidt.

I put the magazine on a shelf near my bed. I'll read that later, I thought. The sight of it triggered a strange physical reaction in me. Reading the article's title and subhead had been . . . a blow to my midsection. A stab to my heart. I couldn't read it right away because it was too painful.

That was in April. The months went by, and eventually I began looking around, thinking I might glance at the article now. I couldn't avoid this case: the papers were full of it; television was full of it. In June I finally found the magazine, just where I'd left it, but now buried under a pile of old family pictures I'd taken out of a cabinet to sort through. Thank you, Dr. Freud.

I made myself a cup of coffee and carried it into the living room. When I opened the magazine to the first paragraph, I read a description of Cara Clausen (now Schmidt) in her hospital room after the baby's birth, holding her newborn daughter, looking at her fingers, cooing to her, calling her "Baby Boo."

I laid the magazine in my lap and looked up at nothing. My first reaction was fragmented and indecipherable. Tiny bits of remembered glimpses impinged on my thoughts. It was as if I were asleep and dreaming, seeming to see the dark head of the baby, if it was *the* baby, in his hospital bassinet, at the door of a cold room—not chilly, but drab and gray. *The* baby—*my* baby, not Cara's.

And for some absurd reason I kept remembering a sleeveless dress I wore in the summer of 1965, six months after the birth of my son, when I was thin again. It was a straight, knit dress—I think we called them sheaths—that I kept pulling up under the belt in back because it was pooched out in the seat. Why that dress? Maybe because it was the one in the pictures of me and Dan—my Dan, not

Dan Schmidt, Baby Clausen's father—that I'd finally thrown away.

As soon as I began to read that magazine article I became Cara Clausen. The reviled, the hated, the demonized Cara. The birth mother who should do the right thing and just disappear, taking her wounded self back where she came from. Out of sight, one day to be—God willing—out of mind. As Judge William F. Ager, Jr., of the Circuit Court for Washtenaw County, Michigan, told Cara and Dan, "Think of the possibility of saying 'Enough.' " If they gave up fighting to get back their child, he said, "People all over the United States would say, 'These people have acted in the best interest of the child.' "

I remembered what my friend Betsy had said months before, when she heard the judge's words repeated on a television show: "When would *I* stop fighting to get back *my* child? *Never.*" Of course, she had never given up her child in the first place. That was Cara Clausen's big mistake. True, she had changed her mind quickly—before a month was out—but it was too late, legally.

My heart went out to Cara—another confused, regretful woman, but old enough, smart enough, strong enough, and lucky enough to set about undoing her mistakes before all the hours and days and weeks and months and years of more than two and a half decades had dwindled down.

All of this Cara Clausen had to do in public, for when the De-Boers were ordered to return Baby Jessica, they had called in the media.

The media responded. Although I did not watch television, everyone I know seemed to have seen a host of programs on which the case was discussed. Just about everyone thought that Cara Clausen was a monster, ripping a toddler away from "the only home she's ever known."

I still have mixed feelings about the case. I do not believe that Baby Jessica, or Anna, can possibly be unscathed. I personally assume that she is in shock, although television networks have shown film footage of her playing happily. However, I blame the DeBoers for stretching out a legal process that took the baby to toddlerhood.

Blame is beside the point, I know. And yet I can't help feeling bitter about the legal battle that so polarized the two camps who adored this child and ended up torturing her.

"The birth mother signed a contract," one friend said in disgust. "She signed it, and that's all there is to it."

"Elaine," I pleaded, "First of all, the 'contract' is different in every state. If she'd been somewhere else the adoption wouldn't even have been final when she changed her mind! Birth mothers are *supposed* to have time to change their minds! It's not some ordinary contract! Try to imagine what it's like to be pregnant and unmarried, mortified at your condition, alone with your shame. Can't you imagine the panic? Can't you imagine making a mistake?" Can't you imagine telling some lies to comfort yourself and tie up the loose ends of your unravelling life? I thought.

Nothing would budge Elaine. "She signed on the dotted line."

Talking on the phone to the adoptive father whom I have previously called "the married man," ten years after the end of our affair, I was surprised at his vehemence when he mentioned Cara Clausen. "She was fine until she fell into the clutches of that insane group!" he shouted.

I moved the receiver away from my ear. He was talking about Concerned United Birthparents, or CUB, whose members had encouraged Cara to fight to get her daughter back. Cara, racked by depression, had gone to her first CUB meeting even before she was healed from giving birth. *The New Yorker* writer identified CUB as "a secretive, radical organization that was founded in 1976 by birth parents who had experienced such devastating pain after placing their babies for adoption that they felt the only way they could go on was to search for them." I found out later how rankling that description was to many birth parents, since CUB was recognized as a legitimate organization by such longstanding agencies as the Child Welfare League of America, but when I read it my thrilled first thought had been, How can I join?

For Cara's sake, I tried to mediate with my more-or-less friend on the phone. "I think she went to CUB because she was already filled with regret at giving up the baby," I ventured.

"They got their claws into her and wouldn't let her quit!" he shrieked.

"I don't think she'd go through what she's going through just to please a bunch of other people," I said. "You don't stand up in public to be humiliated again and again if you don't feel very strongly about your cause. I think she's going by her lights."

"Well, it's horrible," he said. "Horrible! Look at you—*You're* perfectly fine. You don't bellyache all over the place!"

No? I thought. How odd, because I certainly *felt* like bellyaching. But I didn't say that, because I couldn't yet express how I felt about any of this. I just knew that it killed me to read hateful editorials and articles about Cara, and that these seemed to be proliferating in the press.

I wondered if I was as alone as I felt, until one day my neighbor Barbara came upstairs to drop off her daughter to play with Laura. In the kitchen, I told her I was floored by the DeBoer-Schmidt case.

"It's such a sick, sick thing!" she cried. "I mean, what are the DeBoers thinking? What are they going to do when this child asks about her birth parents? Are they going to tell her the truth? 'Your parents loved you so much that they spent years of their lives trying to get you back—but *we kept you!*' Is that what they're going to tell her?"

Barbara, a television hound, went on and on about how the baby looked *exactly* like Dan Schmidt. I hunted for *The New Yorker* and showed her a paragraph about Robby and Jan DeBoer: "During the nights [after taking the baby home], Robby woke frequently, not only to feed Jessica but also to stare at her. 'Jan, she feels like such a part of me,' she said. 'Maybe in some mystical way she *is* mine. Maybe she was just destined to be grown inside another woman's womb.'"

Barbara yelped a laugh but managed to grimace at the same time. "Pu-leeze!"

"I don't know," I admitted. I felt sorry for Robby DeBoer, and I felt that her fantasy was one that might occur to any euphoric adoptive parent. "I'd probably think something like that if I adopted a baby," I mused.

"Yeah, well, denial's great when you want to feel good," Barbara said. "Too bad it has nothing to do with reality."

I knew by now that I wasn't an impartial observer of Cara's case, as I thought of it, but I wasn't sure how I felt about my own. I kept scanning papers and magazines for articles on the subject of adoption, and then I went to a bookstore and bought out their "Adoption" shelf. I began what Gloria Steinem has called "biblio-therapy," reading as much as I could to try to discover, or construct, my point of view. It was as if I were hacking a clearing out of the forest of memories and emotions that crowded my consciousness. It was extraordinarily hard going, particularly in the dim light of the negative view of birth parents expressed by some writers.

In one *New York Times* op-ed article, Elizabeth Bartholet, an adoptive mother whose identification blurb said only that she was a Harvard Law School professor and the author of a book on adop-tion, referred to Dan Schmidt as Jessica's "sperm father." The main thrust of her piece seemed to be to advise the state of Iowa to "revise its laws to provide for termination of the parental rights of putative fathers known and unknown unless they demonstrate their desire and ability to act as parents shortly after the birth of their biological children."

Dan Schmidt's parenthood of Baby Clausen was not putative: it had been established by DNA testing when the baby was five months old. And as to demonstrating his desire to act as a parent shortly after the birth: Dan Schmidt's daughter had been born February 8; he learned that he was a father on February 27; and on March 12, when his daughter, whom Bartholet called "his genetic product," was five weeks old, he filed a motion asking the court to vacate the parental-termination orders. It is difficult for me to imagine anyone acting more quickly.

In the course of arguing that there were too many legal barriers to adoption, Bartholet described a Massachusetts court ruling that returned a boy to biological parents who had tortured him. Then she wrote, "It takes a lot in this country to terminate birth-parent rights and to free children for adoption." To me it seemed incendiary to use such an egregiously horrifying example to make a case for the easing of adoption laws.

I found that whenever I read an article such as Bartholet's, I would lie down for a while afterward. If Laura was at home, I would wait until she was asleep before looking at the *New York Times*. Therapy had given me the tools to recognize when it was time to go back to my psychiatrist, and I knew that the strange exhaustion from which I was now suffering was directly related to my reading. Reading about adoption was making me sick. I needed to talk.

Soon, in a bit of déja vû, I was sitting across from my doctor sobbing out an hour.

I had wondered if my feelings—especially the tremendously negative ones I had toward the adoptive parents who were authoring the articles that sent me to my pillow—might make my psychiatrist uncomfortable, for as it happens she is also an adoptive mother. But apparently they did not. She had often told her own children, who were both now in their early twenties, that she would help them find their birth parents when they wished to search. So far, they hadn't, but the offer stood.

She watched me cry. She listened as I told her that I felt profoundly, inexplicably alone, even though I was surrounded for much of each day by my family, by other mothers, by children and friends.

"You weren't surrounded the first time," she said.

I blew my nose and sighed. The tears stopped.

"Have you thought of writing about these feelings?" she asked.

"Michelle has thought of my writing about them," I told her. "Does that count? And when I'm not nauseous, I think about it, myself," I said. "When I'm not felled by depression and forced to take to my bed, I think about it. When I stop crying, when I—"

My psychiatrist nodded as I reached for another Kleenex. "Maybe now is not the time."

10

I was not angry since I came to France until this instant.
William Shakespeare, *Henry V*

FIFTEEN YEARS EARLIER, when I was in my late twenties and had cryocautery, the doctor warned me that the surgery might inhibit fertility. I was seized with the desire to call the Winnicott Foundation. (I had always assumed that only if I could have another child would I be able to put my son's birth behind me.)

I told the secretary at Winnicott that I wanted a note put in my son's file, saying I was available if he wanted to get in touch with me for any reason.

She answered that while they could put a note in the file, they couldn't give him my name even if he asked. It was against the law.

I was dumbfounded. "Why?"

"Your files were sealed by the court. To protect your privacy."

"But I don't want to be protected," I said.

She offered no condolences.

Ten years after that telephone conversation and two years before Laura was born, my mother died, leaving, among other things, a gold watch to pass along to her grandchild, "if possible."

I called the Winnicott Foundation again. I introduced myself and explained why I was calling.

"The person who deals with birth mothers isn't here right now," said the woman on the other end of the line. I knew she wasn't the same one I'd spoken with years earlier. "I'll have to have her call you back," she said.

"All right," I said, and gave her my number. She asked if I was still at my Seattle address. I gave her my new one, in New York. "What's her name?" I asked.

Her first name was the same as that of my beautiful grandmother (the one Laura resembles).

"I'll remember that," I said.

"She's very busy," I was told, "so it may be a while. But you *will* hear from her."

Although she was businesslike, by the end of this brief exchange the woman on the telephone had begun to warm up. I took heart and asked if she could give me some information—"anything at all."

She put down the phone. I waited.

She picked it up again but didn't speak right away. "Well," she said slowly. She was reading. I had told her his birthday was January 16, 1965. "First of all, his birthday is January 15." And then she told me two things: that my son's parents had taken him to Winnicott Foundation Christmas parties when he was little, and that they had adopted a daughter when he was three.

It was thrilling news, but when I hung up I wasted no time lingering in exultation. Instead, I shifted swiftly to guilt. I was certain that the woman on the phone had broken the rules when she had glanced through my son's file and told me the little she did. I had suborned this witness, and who was I? A snoop. Someone who was supposed to get on with her life.

Over the years, I had found myself unable to relieve myself of my weighty memories. I would forget for months at a time, or even for a year, but there would always come a day when I couldn't. I had always assumed that my experience would diminish in importance as it retreated in time, but I found instead that it was only more focused by the passage of time.

As I grew older, I gradually gained a cruelly clear perspective on what I had done. As I matured enough to think of myself as a possible parent, the ramifications of my youthful act—giving away my child—took on tragic proportions.

I so much wanted to have a child. I was already a mother—a rudimentary one, but a mother—and I may have also felt that only by having another baby openly and legitimately could I come out of the closet and be known as the mother I already, secretly was. I watched each successive boyfriend carefully, wondering what kind of father he would make. Would he check to see if the diaper was wet, hold a hand firmly enough on the subway platform, set an example and wait for the walk light?

At a friend's college graduation when I was twenty-one, some-one's older sister had brought her three-month-old. The baby was sick with a bad cold—stuffy, drippy, miserable. I volunteered to take care of her while everyone else went to a ceremony. I can still remember the feeling of holding her and humming softly to her. I don't know if I would have been so natural with my own child, especially as he grew into a toddler, a kindergartener, an adolescent. Whatever it is that makes one comfortable with newborns and in-fants, something less instinctual and more thoughtful is required to love and direct an older child. I had forfeited that experience.

Most of the time I had few thoughts about him-whose-name-I-did-not-know; I tried to live in the present and tend to my own life and try to improve it and make it a good one. I tried not to look back. I was grateful my son had been adopted through a respected agency, and not through someone who knew someone who knew a lawyer who knew a doctor who knew a pregnant girl whose baby he could "get." My son's parents had been carefully evaluated before they were allowed to adopt—much more than biological parents ever are—and they might also have been interviewed by someone as astute as Linda Cannon Burgess, the author of *The Art of Adoption,* who in fact had been with an agency in the Washington area during the sixties.

Often, to comfort myself, I thought about the two things the woman I spoke with at Winnicott had told me. My son went to Winnicott Foundation Christmas parties: That clearly meant that his parents lived in the Washington area and made themselves part of a larger group of adoptive families. They must have been at ease with the fact of his adoption, and he must have known he was adopted right from the start. Two: they adopted again, when he was three, so they must have been satisfied enough, happy enough with him to want to adopt a second time. And of course there is the implicit approval of them by Winnicott, which blessed the family twice.

My son's parents were wonderful people. That was my simple deduction.

I waited for the Winnicott social worker with the same name as my beautiful grandmother to return my call. I waited for a month, I waited for a year. I waited longer. Did I have the courage to dial Winnicott again? Not until 1994, six years later.

I spent the summer of 1993 upstate in the Catskills, where I worked on illustrations for a children's book I had written for Laura the winter before. I had a deadline to meet. When Harvey was with us I would work on them all day, but he was often in the city. I would wait until after Laura went to bed at night to spend some quiet hours in the pleasurable activity of inventing colorful scenes that included Laura, her two cats, several of her playmates, and a host of close family friends, many of them canine.

When I couldn't work on the pictures—when I was in the back yard watching Laura and her friends—I perused the books I'd found that spring on a shelf marked "Adoption" at a bookstore. I'm grateful that I started with one called *The Adoption Triangle,* by Arthur D. Sorosky, Annette Baran, and Reuben Pannor. It is a model of respect for "the triad"—birth parents, adoptee, adoptive parents.

It was the first time I had considered myself an integral part of the whole business. I'd felt like persona non grata, the fly in the ointment, the fifth wheel that would tip an otherwise perfectly balanced cart. I was so used to thinking of myself as someone who was no longer supposed to exist that whenever I felt an urge to call Winnicott over the years, I had expended enormous amounts of energy keeping myself from dialing, forcing myself to wait out the day, wait out the week, wait out the month—until I became involved in something and forgot, for a while, that I had wanted to call at all. Until I read *The Adoption Triangle,* I was sure I'd never been told that I could ask for reports on my son's progress. I suddenly realized that it was very likely I could have; I may even have been informed of that right, but if so I had forgotten it in my willingness to try to disappear.

When I began reading these newer books, which no longer gave even the shortest shrift to the supposed psychoses of the "unwed mother"—a term blessedly relegated to the past—I realized that I was someone whose existence mattered. I learned that birth parents mattered perhaps most to many adopted children and adults, some of whom were suffering from simple curiosity and some from real longing to connect to their biological roots. Heartened by my new perspective as a member of the triad, I realized that I was almost certainly entitled to the bits of information that Winnicott had given to me. I wondered if it had been possible to ask for a picture of my son. I wondered if it was too late, now, to ask.

As I read, I kept my back to Laura and her playmates, the better to hide my rapidly blinking eyelids. It was interesting to me that, according to the authors of *The Adoption Triangle,* half of the birth parents they interviewed "continued to have feelings of loss, pain, and mourning over the child they relinquished." I could have been in either half of that survey, depending on the year I was queried. More than three-quarters of birth parents expressed interest in a reunion. Nearly ninety percent reiterated that they did not want to hurt the adoptive parents.

The authors wrote,

When our sample of birth parents was asked if they were interested in updating the information about themselves contained in agency case records, 95 per cent responded affirmatively. . . . They would like their children to know that they had 'made it,' are respected citizens in their communities, have their own families, are happily married, and, most important, that they cared about the children they relinquished. A fear of rejection by the agencies was expressed by many when asked why they did not take steps to update their records.

Had I been rejected by Winnicott? What I *felt* was that Winnicott wished I did not exist. Why else had they never responded to my call? I was always listed in the Manhattan telephone directory, so I could not even comfort myself with the thought that the secretary had scrambled my phone number. I felt that it would probably be easier for agencies if after relinquishing their children birth parents simply disappeared, as they traditionally have done. As I had done.

In *The Adoption Triangle,* I learned the many names for birth parents: "first, original, . . . natural, biological, physical, real, true, other, and blood" parents. We were called "biological conceivers" by those who couldn't accord us even the merest claim to the term "parent." But we were above all what the authors sympathetically but bluntly called "the forgotten parents."

I learned that we were rarely forgotten by our offspring, many of whom were tormented by the desire to find us. In the seventies and eighties, when articles about adoptee searches were being published, I didn't read them. Although I am told by friends that I expressed a longing to know about my son, and that I thought of trying to find him, I was still mired in the certainty that I would be only an intruder if I searched for him. I was unwilling to be swept up in a possibly futile search for someone who perhaps did not want to know me and who had been reared by parents who in all likelihood would resent my intrusion.

Having begun this journey, I understand my tentativeness. It is so hard to dredge up the memories and harder to forge into the unknown, where barrier after barrier obstructs your path. It is hard to find the strength to look for someone whom you have never met but never forgotten.

I should have expected some of the books to bring me to my knees, as the many DeBoer / Schmidt editorials had. In *You're Our Child: The Adoption Experience,* authors Jerome Smith, Ph.D., and Franklin I. Miroff included many transcripts of sessions with adoptees and others. In one meeting with a young woman who was hoping to find her birth mother, Smith, a social worker and adoptive parent, counseled her: "This mother may not want to see you and may be upset. . . . She may say . . . 'I look at you as a total stranger.' "

If my son had called me at any point in my life I would have begged him to come right over. I would have hugged him until he gasped for air. I would have taken him to work, to school, to parties, saying, "Meet my son!" For me, the anonymity promised by Winnicott was an imposition on me. It might have meant something to my mother; it might have meant something to the adoptive parents. To me, it was a burden. I wanted to tell the truth, painful or embarrassing or shameful as I felt it to be. It would have been far easier for me to stand up in the light of day if my son had been by my side. "I look on you as a total stranger"—those heartless words would never come from someone like me, and I doubted I could be so terribly different from most other birth mothers. Not all agencies were as fortresslike as Winnicott. Many, I found out gradually, were the primary agents of searches and reunions, whether begun by adoptees or their birth parents—or, in some cases, adopters.

I thought about my son. The authors of *The Adoption Triangle* had mentioned Jean Paton, an adoptee, social worker, author, and open-records advocate who found her birth mother when she was forty-seven. Paton felt that "In the soul of every orphan is an eternal flame of hope for reunion and reconciliation with those he has lost." And another researcher coined the term "geneological bewilderment" to describe the feelings of many adoptees as they ponder their heritage. In *Secrets,* Sissela Bok says, "Consider the experience of children . . . who know that they have been adopted, but are told that the identity of their biological parents must remain secret. They live with a secret that concerns their very identity, but cannot reach to its center, nor understand why it should be kept from them."

Did my son know anything about me, or about his birth father? Did his parents remember what they were told about us? Did they remember it years later, when the baby was no longer a baby, but old enough to ask? Had he even wanted to ask? Had he felt entitled to ask? Would it make him feel ungrateful to his parents to ask about his others? If he ever asked about me, was he told that the records were sealed for my protection? I could only hope that no one had discouraged him if he had shown curiosity about me.

Dr. Smith finally asked one birth mother, "What does it take to completely sever those ties, do you have any idea?"

My response would be to ask, "Do you think those ties *should* be completely severed?"

But the young woman in the interview answered forthrightly: "I don't think you can."

Several couples I knew well adopted children when I was in my twenties and thirties, and I knew that times had changed. I heard about open adoptions, foreign adoptions, private adoptions. I also knew that the increased openness and strengthened position of birth mothers frightened many adoptive parents. One friend of mine, knowing my history and also knowing how much I loved children, told me that instead of the usual honorary aunt, I could be her two adoptees' honorary birth mother.

"I trust you, Peggy," she said, laughing nervously. "I'd feel safer if it was you."

Safer. Safe from their *actual* birth mother? Safe from the worrying thought that blood might prove thicker than love? I think my friend was simply like me—afraid of the unknown.

There is less of that unknown these days, when birth parents can choose adopters for their child, some even insisting on knowing the adopters' names, addresses, and telephone numbers. I do not think that most adoptions, however, involve full disclosure. I know a couple on the East Coast who found a suitable birth mother through an advertisement, which is how the majority of adopters find children today. The birth mother-to-be was from a western state; she had one child, whose father had died, and the man she married on the rebound from her widow's grief had abandoned her when she became pregnant. She wanted to give up their child, but she was determined to know as much as she could about the family the baby would be joining. The prospective adoptive couple agreed that the birth mother could call their brothers, sisters, parents—the baby's uncles, aunts, and grandparents-to-be. But when the prospective adopters told their family members to expect her calls, they begged them to be careful not to tell the birth mother where they lived. "Don't mention Montclair," they would say. "Whatever you do, don't give her an area code or a last name!"

The summer of my reading binge, I ran across an article titled "Baby Hunt" in *New York Magazine*. The author, Dorothy Kalins, described her search for a child, which had begun with ads designed to attract a birth mother. Their lawyer, Stanley Michelman, whom Kalins called "the dean of the nation's adoption lawyers," suggested "we install a separate, unlisted telephone to isolate the calls from birth mothers and to protect our identities."

I wrote in the margin: *Plus ça change.*

One day, instead of working on my children's-book illustrations, I wrote a short column about how painful it was to be a birth mother from the deep-dark-secret years, and how hard it was to know nothing about the child I had given up. I sent the piece off to the *New York Times*'s "Hers" column editor. Then, standing by the mailbox at our small-town, upstate post office, I found myself stiff with anxiety. What if they published it?

My situation was different than it had been when I was a single woman. Now I was hardly able to consider this subject without having to sit down and recover my equilibrium. How could I write publicly about something I could barely stand to think about? And what about Laura? Wouldn't a "Hers" column generate a few congratulations that would have to be explained? There was also the problem of tears. Whenever I opened one of the books on adoption and began to read, I cried. Would I cry if a mother in the park said she'd read my piece—or, worse, looked at me funny? Again, the closet looked good to me—risk-free and easy. Each time I dealt with my past, I ricocheted between resolve and retreat, and each time the direction I had taken last looked wrong.

Linda Cannon Burgess, the author of *The Art of Adoption,* is a social worker who was an adoption counselor for many years. Before writing her book, Burgess had looked up many of the adoptees whose placements she made. While her book is both a plea for adoptees' rights to open records and an appraisal of the positive and negative sides of adoptive couples, adoptees, birth parents, birth grandparents, and adoption itself (she remained strongly in favor of it, on the whole), I found myself focusing on her message of the importance of genetic heritage.

"In returning to observe adoptees after years in their adoptive homes," she wrote, "I have seen that they are still largely the offspring of their biological parents, not only in outward appearance but in their interests and character. I don't have answers, only observations. They show me that an adoptive environment may modify development but does not change the essential nature with which the adoptee is born."

To me, so invisible even to myself until recent months, it was as if I were discovering further confirmation of my existence. There was a strong possibility, I saw, that I might exist as an important person not only in the eyes of the Winnicott Foundation, but also in my son. I felt substantial. I felt *real*. Everywhere I looked in Burgess's book, I found evidence for my reality, and even for my influence (if only genetic) in my son's development. It gave me a heady feeling. Since my son's birth, it had occasionally dawned on me that without birth parents adoption would not exist, but until I read Burgess's book, I had never managed to parlay that revelation into pride.

Burgess remained solidly on the side of the children whom she placed—not their parents, birth or adoptive—as she argued their right to the information kept in sealed files, holding that their self-knowledge superseded the desire of any other party for the comforts of privacy or denial.

"The strongest argument social workers raise against the search," she wrote, "is the shock a birth mother may suffer from confrontation with an offspring, long buried in her past. Probably she will have married and had other children. She may have established a conforming way of life for herself, separate from and incompatible with her youthful transgression. She may have kept the secret from her husband." The very experienced Burgess knew better. "Contrary to public surmise, birth mothers' repudiation of their returning offspring is exceptional. . . . Confronted by reunion, mothers are likely to be more emotionally touched than their returning offspring."

At the end of the book, I found that Burgess was strict on the subject of opening records to birth parents: "Their search lacks the justification which that of the adopted person possesses. It is understandable on an emotional level but as a civil rights issue such a search is not well grounded. The prior relinquishment of parental rights made voluntarily is forever binding."

It was a harsh view, and I was taken aback for a moment. Like many birth mothers, I had been a minor. A minor is not considered to be capable of informed consent to many things, including marriage. It seems very strange to me that I could legally agree to sign away my rights to my child, while without my mother's co-signature I could not make that child legitimate.

In my own case I knew that I had been in a state something like suspended animation—suffering from dissociated feelings, unable to deal with the grief I had been bottling up since my father's death or with the family problems caused by my sister's mental illness. I have always had an ability to smile on cue and speak with confidence in almost any social situation. I never was at a loss for words. And yet *no matter how mature I was or seemed at sixteen, I was only sixteen.* To me it seems unjust that I should be bound by my looping, childish signature.

Finally, reading Burgess's book, the words that struck me most strongly were: "I have never heard adopters speak of 'the mother you don't know.' Perhaps for the parents the expression conjures up the uncomfortable image of the mother you might know—someday."

One night at bedtime, I read the story of Sleeping Beauty, Disney version, to Laura, who startled me by asking if Princess Aurora's mommy was sad when the good fairies took her baby daughter away.

"Very sad," I said.

"*You* would sure be sad!" Laura extrapolated.

"I would never let someone take you away, no matter what," I answered.

Laura ignored that and went on musing about the fairy tale and how we would feel as its characters. "Well," she said after much thought, "I know that whoever it was would take good care of me until you got me back. I would be adopted, right?"

For form's sake, and because optimism is important, I agreed with Laura. I hugged her and kissed her hair. I did not point out that adoption is forever, that a child, once taken away by good fairies, might never see her first mother again. She might even forget there had been another mother. She might forget she could know her again—someday.

11

*I want to find myself, learn my human name—simple things
that the people of Gotham take for granted.*

The Penguin, in "Batman Returns"

LAURA SAID, I know where I came from. Where? I ask her. Your belly, Silly, remember? It is simple for her.

My search, if that is what this halting process of discovery is all about, became, for me, an attempt to reconcile past and present, the truth of my experience with the truths of others. When I began writing the book about Sally and me, I found that I could hardly bear the memories. Writing that book was like going through analysis for hours a day, dredging and sifting and trying to come to some sense of peace. In the end, having more or less succeeded, I was grateful for the chance to have molded a new understanding out of old material, and that gratitude enabled me, finally, to pick up the pieces of this other story and try to see what I could see.

In the prospective "Hers" column I had written, "Do you know my baby, now twenty-nine?" Because I understood by then what I was trying to do.

One night in August, after finishing Burgess's book, I dried my tears, washed my face, sat down by the phone, and dialed New York City information to ask for the number of that "radical, secretive" group, Concerned United Birthparents. No number. I tried the outlying boroughs. No number. Finally, I called Iowa information. Iowa was where Cara Clausen joined CUB. I had a vague memory that their headquarters were in that state.

"Hold for the number," the operator sang.

I held, I wrote the number on the flyleaf of Burgess's book, and then I wondered, Do I really want to get into all this?

Did I have a choice? I dialed the number and the phone was answered immediately by a woman. I told her I was a birth mother and that I'd heard of CUB through *The New Yorker* article on the Schmidt-DeBoer case.

After I explained that I was looking for a son I had given up nearly three decades before, she gave me the name of a group in New York run by a man named Sam Friedman. Friedman also ran a search-and-support group called Contact. Because my son was adopted in Washington, she gave me the name of a birth mother in that area, Becca Dietz, who might know something about Winnicott.

"Have you registered with Soundex?" she asked.

"Soundex?"

"In Nevada. The International Soundex Reunion Registry."

I had heard of the ALMA registry. Was that what she meant?

"No. This one is free."

I took down the address.

It was late. Frogs were chirping and moths were convening by the streetlights. I sat on a blue-and-white upholstered straight-backed chair that had belonged to my late aunt and thought about family ties. I was unprepared for the conversation I was now having, because I had confidently expected to get no answer at the number I'd impulsively dialed. Surely even with the time change, it was too late for anyone to answer an office phone. I now felt as if I were slipping down a steep bank and into a stream whose current could sweep me away.

The woman on the other end of the line, out in Iowa, where, I thought, the sky was probably still light, talked in a cheerful, informative voice, telling me about the springtime marches from New York to Washington led by Friedman, who was an adoptee. It was from her I learned that CUB, rather than being a radical, secretive group, was an established organization recognized by the Child Welfare League of America, among others.

I laughed.

"You'll get used to stuff like that," she said. Then, possibly hearing the uneasiness that lay behind my silence, "—if you *do* decide to get involved."

"Oh, I'm involved," I assured her blithely. "I'm writing about it."

"Great," she said. She sounded as if she believed me, and why shouldn't she? I believed myself.

After we hung up, I went to my desk and sat down. I made a note to call Sam Friedman the next day to ask about his support group, and I wrote to Becca Dietz, asking her how to search in Washington, D.C.

I also sent a note to the International Soundex Reunion Registry asking how I could put my name in their files. The CUB representative had said that if my birthson was also registered, Soundex would send us each other's names, addresses, and telephone numbers.

Upstairs later, I tiptoed in to check on Laura, newly four, who since her birthday the week before was looking suddenly much older.

I pulled a blanket over her and went to my room.

As I undressed, I wished I'd called Harvey in the city, where he was working, to say goodnight. I didn't go back downstairs to the telephone. I just whispered goodnight into the dark.

As I put my head down I thought of something he and I often said to each other, and I whispered that, too: "Thank you for the daughter."

Then I thanked God again. Thank you for the daughter, God.

I did not say a word about my son. I was feeling closer, but I was afraid to mention him. I wanted to be sure to thank God for the blessing in the hand, and not ask for too much with regard to the one in the bush, whose other mother might at this very minute be thanking God herself.

Gradually I discovered there was a lot of down time in this search business, much of it of my own devising. I found myself subtly balking. Before the week was out I received an information packet from Contact, Sam Friedman's search-and-support group, along with a calendar of meeting times, and I duly looked them over, but after circling a date that was coming up soon, I put the Contact schedule away in a file folder without marking my own calendar. It was to be eight months before I finally made it to one of those meetings.

I was to learn that such halting progress is common. I could not muster the self-confidence to move ahead except in fitful bursts, separated by long periods of vagueness and inertia. I was afraid of calling Winnicott, in case they once again failed to respond. I was afraid to join a search organization, in case I failed to find my birthson. I was afraid to join in case I *did* find him and discovered that he was someone for whom I felt nothing, or, worse, someone I did not like. I was afraid to search in case I found my son and he was someone I would love the way I loved my Laura. I was afraid my heart would break to think of all the years when I had not known him. I was afraid to search in case I loved him and he had no feelings for me, or for Laura, his half-sister, or any interest in meeting us. Laura would care about that; Laura would care about him. Laura cared about family, and we had such a small one. Finally, I was afraid to search in case my birthson had died.

Why, I wondered, did I need to disrupt my days and nights, thinking about something that might never be resolved? Why did I need to do anything but enjoy my family and my work?

I would find out again and again that I just had to explore that wilderness, try to map it, and then find a navigable route through it, instead of imagining the worst, or the best, or anything at all. But I also needed to stop and rest and reconnoiter and look back at where I had been, before I could move on toward the dragons lurking in the mists that lay beyond the terra firma of anything I already knew.

In the fall, it was time for Laura to begin another year of nursery school. This time, like the year before, I was the last parent to leave the classroom. I knew from experience that when I finally made the break Laura would be fine. I could see that her part of our separation problem was normal and finite. It was my own half that was neurotic and ongoing, but I finally decided that I could make the break.

"I'm not going to stay today, Pumpkin," I told Laura at the beginning of the second week. She began to cry but, significantly, didn't argue about going to school. She chose what she wanted to wear and picked out a necklace that, she said, "would also look nice." I know a transition object when I see one, so I complimented the jewelry, helped her pull on her clothes, and got us out the door. When I left her with her teachers, I told them I'd pick her up at the end of the day. Then I kissed her. She cried a little, but she didn't cling. Then I went home.

To my surprise, I found that I was all right, too. It was a breakthrough, and I wasn't entirely surprised. I had come to understand that my distress over leaving Laura had something to do with "losing" my first baby. Armed with that interpretation, I was able, finally, to see the obvious: Laura was not the boy I left behind me; she was the girl I would pick up at two o'clock sharp. The truth had set me . . . maybe a little bit freer, just for now. I knocked on wood.

Again I began to vacillate on what I had started calling "this birth mother business." When I received a registration form from Soundex the first week in October, I filled it in with my name, the birth father's name, the hospital, date, and time of birth, and sent it back with a stamped, self-addressed envelope. *I was on!*

Two weeks later, when my "Hers" column was rejected, I found to my surprise that I was relieved. I stuffed it into a drawer. *Off.* I wasn't ready to come out.

I got a call from a birth mother in New York named Marianne, to whom Becca Dietz, in Maryland, had given my name. *On.* She had found her son years before; she rarely went to Sam Friedman's support-group sessions any more, but she offered to go with me my first time and introduce me to Sam. I thanked her, took her number, and told her I'd call her in a week or two. I dropped the slip of paper bearing her number in a file folder I had marked "nice girl" (as in "a nice girl like me"), where I had begun keeping all the odds and ends—magazine articles, newspaper clippings, addresses, brochures—associated with this birth mother business.

Then I forgot about it. *Off.*

Almost overnight I found my stamped, self-addressed envelope from the Soundex registry in my own mailbox, postmarked Carson City, Nevada.

I carried the letter into the elevator. My heart ratcheted quickly through several beats. I was actually frightened, because of my father's heart attack. I felt as if my chest held a pummeling fist. My face flushed and my ears began to ring. At the door of the apartment, I tore open the envelope. It was a form letter.

> Dear Registrant:
> Your registration was received here October 2, 1993.
> ISRR [the International Soundex Reunion Registry] will contact you directly only when a match occurs with another registration received.
> Updated information that will help us to determine a relationship is welcome and please maintain your current address with this registry.
> Thank you and best wishes.
> Sincerely,
> Anthony S. Vilardi,
> Registrar

Until I opened that envelope, I had thought of myself as being on the fence as far as searching was concerned, and I was to feel that ambivalence again many times during the next year and more. But at the moment when I took the note out and realized that it was merely a confirmation of my registration, and not a match—that there was no other name and address in the envelope, for my son was not registered with Soundex—I was devastated by disappointment.

I opened the door and closed it again behind me quickly. I went to my bed and crawled under the covers and wept until it was time to leave to get Laura from school, and that was how I found out how much I had hoped for the person I wanted to know to want to know me too.

It is hard to understand how much you love someone you have never met. It is hard to know how much *to* love someone you have never met. I got up, filed the Soundex note in the "nice girl" file, and shut the cabinet drawer.

Michelle kept saying, "Peggy, you've got to do that book."

"I can't do it if I have to lie down every time I think about it, Michelle."

"Oh, you're exaggerating."

"No I'm not."

Besides the pain of dredging up my hard memories, I had another problem. I was worried about Laura and how this might affect her. There would come a time when I would tell her this story—how could a mother not tell a daughter this story?—but whenever I tried to piece together a narrative, I could not imagine the words to tell my little girl that she not only was not my first baby but that I gave the first away. It was a terrible secret to keep, but no matter how I constructed my explanation—I was too young to be a Mommy and I wanted him to have grown-up parents who could take good care of him—it contained that hard pit of news: Your mother was capable of giving away her child. I didn't want Laura to watch her step. I was reluctant to make her more fearful than she had to be anyway, living in a big American city in the late twentieth century. I could put it off for now—I *would* put it off for years—but sooner or later Laura would be entitled to the information that she had a half-brother.

I knew it would be easier to tell Laura about my birth son if I could tell her something about him that would make him real, as an adult, and not leave her with the image of him as the baby I gave up. I wished I could bring the story up to date—out of the sad, lost past and into the present, where possibilities bloomed. I wanted to tell her about her half-brother and then be able to say, ideally, *And here he is!* Barring that best of all possible worlds, it would help if I could tell her that he was all grown up and had his own life, and perhaps she might meet him someday. It took me a long time and a lot of telephone calls before I would realize that at the very least I wanted to be able to tell Laura that her half-brother was alive.

The whole thing was just too wrenching. I couldn't conceive of what would make it worth my while to remember and regret and search. Later I would find out, but, for the time being, I gave it up.

That was October.

One Monday afternoon the following May, I opened the "nice girl" file, looked at the Contact calendar, and called Sam Friedman's number. Yes, there was a meeting that night. I called Harvey, asked him to babysit, and told Laura I had a meeting.

Each step I took, forward or backward, was dictated by impulse. Only later would I grasp the underlying reasons for my actions. It is easy to see how the lack of a match at Soundex caused me to step back. But I never figured out what propelled me forward. Without conscious thought, I would open a drawer, take out a schedule, and go to a meeting. Without conscious thought, I would get back to the path that might, someday, lead to my birth son.

Leaving the house at five-thirty that evening, I strode purposefully to the subway station at Broadway and Seventy-second Street. There I began a confused odyssey in which I dazedly, erroneously sampled various lines of an underground system—east side, west side, all around the town—which for fifteen years I had navigated frequently and easily. At 7:05 I reached the address printed on the Contact brochure. It was an apartment house almost directly across town from mine; I could have taken a bus and been there in fifteen minutes.

The doorman glanced at the paper in my hand and waved me to the elevator. When I reached the door I was looking for, it was ajar. I knocked and walked into a room that was lined with books, half-filled with folding chairs, and dominated by a large desk holding stacks of leaflets and order forms for books and brochures. There was a cash box, and a sign giving the rates for the evening's session: ten dollars for members, fifteen dollars for nonmembers.

A plump, middle-aged man with prematurely white hair called out a welcome. There was only one other person there, a young, handsome, fair-haired man with a tortured expression who tried to smile at me when I came in but was unable to carry it off.

I sat down.

"I'm Sam, and this is Mark. He recently found."

I told them my name and that I'd heard about the meetings from

CUB. I also said I'd been in touch with Becca Dietz.

"Use Becca for search help—she's near D.C. and she'll know more about the agency and the area—and come here to deal with your feelings," Sam said. I asked if there was a birth mothers' group in Manhattan. Sam said he didn't know.

It seemed odd to me that someone whose life and career revolved around members of the adoption triad would not know that, but I didn't give it another thought. I was more disturbed by his brushing off my request for search help. Surely other birth parents and adoptees had found one another from across great distances. I made a mental note to ask Marianne (the one whose number I had dropped in the "nice girl" file and then forgotten) about using ALMA instead, the registry and search organization founded by Florence Fisher.

As Mark sat stiffly and talked to Sam about how he felt about finding his birth mother, his adoptive parents' reaction to his search, and how torn he was, I thought of a million questions to ask. I wanted to know when and how he had finally decided to search, but when I tried to ask, Sam cut me off. "We let people get it all out without interruption," he said. "We don't question each other here. We just express our own 'I' feelings." I knew that many support groups were run on the same principles—no "crosstalk" and no commentary on anyone's feelings but one's own, but it was hard to bite my tongue.

Other people began to arrive. Most of them, like Mark, were very young—late teens, early twenties. Most were exceptionally attractive, physically. I couldn't help thinking of them as products of men and women who had found each other irresistible. Like Hester Prynne's daughter Pearl, they seemed "the unpremeditated offshoots of a passionate moment." I found myself searching their young faces, imagining that each one was my child. I was shaken to see their corporeal solidity, their reality, their *size*—as if I had never quite believed that the baby I relinquished would grow up.

I was the only birth mother there.

An adoptee who had been searching for his birth mother for most of his life, Sam was a no-nonsense kind of guy, whose speech was speckled with expletives, but his handling of each person at the meeting was respectful and often insightful.

Mark spoke first, announcing to the group that he had found his birth mother. He talked about tracing her parents first, and that when he had called them they had told him angrily not to call their daughter—that she would not want to meet him: she was married now and had never told her husband. Then Mark laughed. "I called her anyway, and the first thing she did was yell to her husband to come to the phone—he'd always known about me—and then she asked me where I was—if I was close enough to come over."

Mark had met her the following Saturday. As he described his feelings on meeting her, his voice became very soft and his speech became halting, as if he were unable to put the experience into words. "I wanted, I wanted, to—to curl up—in, in her lap, I guess," he finally said. Mark looked like a college football player, strong and handsome and virile. His words were the words of a child—a very small child, one Laura's age. My chest hurt. I wanted to gather him onto my lap the way I would have gathered Laura, to hold him and rock him and rest my lips on his hair, and tell him I loved him and that it would be all right. I wanted him to be my son. I would have settled for Mark. I would have settled for any of the adoptees at the meeting. I would have settled for an end to this.

"My adoptive parents are furious," Mark said, abruptly returning to the present. "I actually think I know how they feel. I was angry all my life, especially every year on my birthday, but nobody ever put two and two together. I feel bad for them, but. . . ." Mark shrugged.

Another adoptee said that after she found her birth mother she seemed to be unable to get along with her adoptive parents and her birth mother at the same time. "It's as if I have to choose, emotionally," she said. "When I love my adoptive parents, I can't stand my birthmom's voice. When I'm close to her, everything my parents say drives me up a wall."

One adoptee mentioned finding a birth mother who was miraculously alive, although the adoptive parents had said she was killed in a car accident. "Yeah," snickered another. "That would be the same

accident that killed *my* birthmom. The one who's alive and well
in Cincinnati."

To them, their adoptive parents' subterfuge was just one more
way to hold on to a child who was not *really* theirs. I did not share
their apparent contempt for the lie that had hurt them, even though
I am generally against lying. I thought the story had probably been
conceived as a kindness. It seemed reasonable to me that adoptive
parents might be unable to imagine how a woman could give up her
baby, and the parents had made up a perfectly plausible explanation.
Only from the grave would your mother allow you, my beloved, to
be separated from her.

I was thinking that many biological parents, myself above all,
would stoop to anything to keep hold of our children, the ones who
are not *really* ours. Our children do not belong to us. We must allow
them to grow up, to separate from us, to become functional adults.
I know that, but do I accept it? Not entirely. I prefer to model myself
on the example of my friend Sandy, whose three adult sons, one with
a wife, live within a two-block radius of her home. I kind of liked the
lie about the dead birth mother.

It was nearly nine o'clock. People kept arriving. The room was
full.

An adoptee not much younger than I was kept glancing at me.
When he spoke, he sounded uncertain about his goals. He loved his
adoptive parents very much, but he longed to find his birth mother.
Yet it didn't sound as if he was carrying out a systematic search. Like
me, many of the adoptees at the meeting seemed vague about their
purpose. Some had never asked their adoptive parents for information about agencies, doctors, or any other possible source of information—they had never taken the first step. Their passivity was
agonizing to witness, and I found their modest, unsuccessful ges-
tures—such as Mother's Day ads in the "personals" columns of local
newspapers—*pathetic.*

Sam understood their reluctance. He knew that they in all likelihood felt rejected by their birth mothers; that they were uncertain
how they would be received if they searched, uncertain what kind of

woman they would find, and afraid of complicating their lives. As a birth mother, I felt sure that many of their birth mothers had not even seen them, were now yearning for reunion, and would welcome them with open arms. Sam, on the other hand, knew that an adoptee also can be afraid to upset his adoptive parents, sometimes out of a sense of gratitude, but often out of an unconscious or semi-conscious fear of being rejected a second time. Sam knew that adoptees whose parents were ambivalent or negative about their search were afraid to risk the parents they had to find the ones they had lost.

Search, search! I wanted to say. But if I had told them honestly how hard it was for me to go forward, wouldn't these adoptees have found my insecurity as painful and pathetic as I found theirs? In that room, there wasn't one person who didn't yearn to be found. A lot of us, however, were finding it very hard to search.

Sam had a theory: A search is a gift to the person who is found. That person may not be ready to accept the gift, but it is nonetheless essential to offer it. I felt that if the gift could be called, say, genetic knowledge, or characterized as, say, the solution to a mystery, it would be easier for all of us to just go ahead and give it and look upon rejection as a comparatively minor disappointment, and not a rejection of us, ourselves. Many of us were so burdened by the fear of rejection we could barely inch forward.

Abruptly, Sam looked at me and asked me how I felt. I was all right, I said. Moved by some stories, interested in others. I admitted that being there was bringing back a lot of memories. I didn't say that the memories were threatening to make me faint.

They flashed in vivid, visual licks—a window, a tube, a pen, a look—but I seemed to feel them in my heart, in my ears, in my legs, behind my eyes. The memory of my obstetrician's redhaired nurse, who conveyed a mixture of curiosity, discomfort, and sympathy, flashed across my mental screen and was gone, as if a strobe had illuminated her image: My chest hurt. Years before, my therapist had mentioned uncried tears as a possible cause of chest pains. I had been doubtful, but eventually I learned that if I cried my heart out I could escape the physical twinges.

This time, I felt no need to cry. I was all right. Fine, thanks.

When I tried to say so a second time, I burst into tears. Whoops. Maybe not all right.

"I'm overwhelmed," I sobbed. My chest stopped hurting.

The meeting went on, and I recovered. The first words are always the hardest. The first words, interrupted by the first tears. I had seen that time and again in my sibling group at the Alliance for the Mentally Ill: tears first, then speech.

Others spoke, all of them adoptees, and I began to learn about the stigma of adoption, which had somehow never occurred to me. I had assumed that the stigma applied only to me. After all, I was the only one hiding, wasn't I? And then it occurred to me that one reason adoptive couples sometimes try to find a "matching" child— someone from parents who are physically similar to themselves—is not just so the child will feel comfortable and less different from the parents, but also so they can pretend the child is biologically theirs. That kind of pervasive lie is bound to emanate from some kind of shame, I guess. And now I was hearing that some adoptees were teased as children. They were taunted by children who called them "unwanted." Some felt humiliated as adults each time they went to a new doctor and were asked for a medical history. Some hated mirrors, wondering always, Whom do I look like? Hearing those beautiful, handsome, talented, accomplished people express their pain made me afraid that my son might be anguished.

I also discovered that although these adoptees longed to know their birth parents, some also felt rage at their abandonment. Their anger was an unwelcome revelation to me. I felt it as an ever-present accusation. When I heard an adoptee wonder if his mother "tried to abort me," or when I heard another ask, "How could she have given away her own child?" I felt myself withdrawing emotionally. I didn't think I could stand the guilt. I didn't think I deserved it. I felt that I had suffered so much, that exploring my own suffering had produced even more of it, and that reaching out into the unknown was terrifying. How could I offer my gift if it would be received with anger?

At one point, someone mentioned a Long Island man, adopted,

who had been accused of murdering nearly a score of prostitutes. He kept talismans from his victims—a driver's license, a piece of jewelry—that were found in his room after his arrest. In the newspapers, there had been the usual letters from adoptive parents and adoption agencies saying that for reporters to have mentioned the fact of the suspect's adoption at all was to stigmatize adoptees and the institution of adoption. At the meeting, however, another point of view prevailed: That in killing whores, the man had been subconsciously killing his birth mother, a woman he may have assumed was at best sexually irresponsible and at worst a prostitute. In storing keepsakes from these anonymous women he was attempting to prevent their leaving, or abandoning, him, in much the same way Jeffrey Dahmer, another serial killer, kept keepsakes—even body parts— and explained his grisly habit by saying of his victims that he "didn't want them to go."

It made sense to adoptees in the room that this young man would harbor such powerful fury and desire toward his birth mother. That was shocking to me. I had to speak.

"I thought I had done the right thing for my son," I said. "I never thought that giving him up could possibly be wrong for *him*. I was always told that he could have a better life if only I gave him up for adoption. I always thought *I* was the problem, the only thing standing between him and a happy life with loving, grown-up parents who had the resources to raise a child."

Sam nodded supportively, but there was no response in the room.

I suppose that those of us who go to groups will eventually understand one another's pain, but I was prevented by the angry atmosphere in the room from speaking up and saying what to me seemed essential: *You cannot imagine what life was like in the pre-Roe v. Wade era. You cannot imagine what your mother went through. You clearly cannot imagine that it was her pregnancy that was not wanted, not you—not her child.* I certainly could not say what I knew in my heart: that the pain I possessed would be negligible if I'd aborted a handful of dividing cells that were quickly, inside me, becoming someone I could not keep, but would never forget.

I came away from the meeting with much on my mind. I also came away with a book: *The Other Mother,* by Carol Schaefer. I wept as I read it, unavoidably reminded of the stunned, solitary girl who was myself at sixteen. In the eighteen years between her pregnancy and her search for the son she gave up, Schaefer had unconsciously buried many of the details of her own story, which surfaced only as she researched and wrote her book. Her story was agonizing to read: her beloved boyfriend's refusal to marry her, her forgiving him, going through the birth alone, nursing her baby in the hospital, giving him up, returning to college, learning to lie, learning to live.

In *The Other Mother,* Schaefer described half a dozen times when she had felt inexplicable but powerful concern about her son. Not long after his birth she and the baby's birth father both had strong suspicions that something was wrong with their son. Eighteen years later she discovered that he had been adopted not once but twice, and that he was taken from his first adoptive home to his second just when she had experienced misgivings about his well-being. And although Schaefer had been told by the adoption agency that her son would be placed out of state, she continually felt a strong sense of his presence whenever she drove to a nearby city. She could not shake the feeling, and later she discovered that he in fact had been adopted, and was living, there.

Some people might snort over such coincidences and dismiss them as just that, but I did not, in part because in reading her book I nearly fell off my chair with shock at one small and fairly insignificant part of her story.

When I was first married and living in Seattle, there was a commercial on television that Christmas season—1971—for a cologne called "Skinny Dip." In it the actress Sandy Duncan, with her pixie haircut, swims upward through water and emerges fresh and sparkling above the surface. "Skinny Dip . . . makes a girl feel pretty," goes the jingle. I can still sing it.

The first time I saw the ad I was *gripped* by it. I saw it two or three more times, and then I went to a beauty parlor. My hair, left to its own devices throughout the late sixties, was a thick, curly mass that fell nearly to my elbows. When I walked it marched to a different drummer, heaving its independent weight along with me while remaining slightly aloft.

"Trim?" asked the hairdresser.

"No," I said. "This short." I held my thumb and forefinger an inch apart.

"Whoopee!"

After an hour and a half of chopping and trimming, she asked if I wanted her to bag my hair, to save it. I left it on the floor. I probably could have sold it, there was so much and it was so long.

My entire upper body was cold for weeks, but I did indeed feel pretty—lighter by far. Reborn, really.

And for years and years and years I remembered that Skinny Dip commercial as if it were *Miracle on Thirty-fourth Street,* and I was always amazed to find that when I mentioned it for some reason— say, in a conversation about Sandy Duncan—no one else recalled it. How could they have missed it—that spellbinding triumph of advertising?

After Carol Schaefer had graduated from college, she moved to New York City and took a job in an advertising agency. She was still so shaken by her experience of pregnancy and relinquishment that after a date she would find herself "in an enormous depression" because she couldn't tell the men she met who she was—"a mother." It was Schaefer's line—"Makes a girl feel pretty"—that became the jingle for the Skinny Dip commercial. How did one birth mother speak to another? Duncan's emergence from water, naked—a birth. The short hair—a woman as infant; or maybe a woman as a young tomboy—sexlessly, safely prepubescent. And "feeling pretty"— something trivial, perhaps, in the eternal scheme of things, but something difficult and complicated for Schaefer and for me because of the dissonance between the word's youthful connotations and our own maturing experiences, and because of the tension between our appearance and the complex truth of who we felt ourselves to be— pretty young women on the surface and brokenhearted mothers underneath. Whatever the reasons, I am convinced that I responded to the Skinny Dip commercial the way that I did because I picked up some subliminal message that Schaefer had unconsciously put in it.

After the first meeting at Sam Friedman's, I was unenthusiastic, to say the least, about searching for someone who might possibly add to the discomfort I already felt. It stopped me in my tracks to see how separately we members of the triad carried our individual sorrows and how blind we were to one another's pain. I was shocked that the adoptees for the most part had never imagined their birth mother's predicament, but eventually I had to admit that I hadn't imagined that my birthson might have been scarred by his experience. When adoptees talked about the primal wound of separation from the biological parent whose blood had nurtured them in the womb, I froze. I had never thought of anyone, really, but myself—my very young, fragile self (I thought forgivingly)—until I met other young, fragile selves at Contact. I felt ashamed that I had grown into my forties without realizing that there were other griefs besides mine. I wondered if anyone had warned me that my child might never get over what I was supposed to put behind me. I thought I knew the answer to that.

Meanwhile, even as chastened and reluctant as I felt, I noticed that I was paradoxically more active for a while. I called Marianne, apologized for going to the meeting without her, and made plans to get together with her at the next one. I asked her about ALMA.

"They hate birth mothers at ALMA."

I didn't question Marianne's opinions or those of anyone else at this stage, because I still didn't know much about searching. I was collecting points of view, and Marianne's was firmly held, so I assumed she knew more than I did. However, I had problems with her style. I felt rushed by her. She paid lip service to my searching at my own pace, but there was always something urgent in her voice—as there often is in my own—and I found myself resisting.

When I told Marianne that my son's adoption went through Winnicott, she sounded as if she'd spat into the phone. They were horrible, the Winnicott people, absolutely *horrible*—the stories she could tell me! Oh, how awful for me, that it was Winnicott! Her harsh words were in keeping with my own judgment of the agency whose birth-mother counselor had never called me back. I had angry, bitter feelings toward Winnicott, and I remembered, too, that in one search guide, Winnicott was the example given for agencies that were hard to crack—I think it was called the "Citadel of agencies." Despite Marianne's hysterical tone, everything she said dovetailed with my own inchoate suspicions.

By the time Marianne arrived, very late, at the next meeting I was feeling resentful. Not of her; of the others in the room. I had begun to feel that some of the complaints I was hearing were not caused by adoption. It reminded me of people in the Alliance for the Mentally Ill meetings who said, for instance, that their mentally ill siblings were resentful of their successes, or that their mentally ill mothers called them too often to ask when they were going to visit. Didn't they know that people who'd never heard of mental illness had jealous siblings and demanding mothers? And didn't adoptees know that even biological children spend half their adolescence wishing their real parents would appear on the scene and save them from the imposters who were ruining their lives? Of course not. That's what made it so sad. And here I was, connecting every affliction in my romantic or reproductive life to my birth motherhood. I'd had it. With all of us.

In two short meetings, I had gone from deeply moved to deeply grumpy. That's when Marianne arrived.

She had a lot to say, some of it about how adoptees don't realize the kind of pain a search dredges up for the birth mother, especially if she's been found without having searched herself. It takes time to get through the feelings, Marianne said, and I was grateful to her for raising that issue.

But then Marianne went on, developing her point into a thundering tirade that Sam tried to moderate only to the extent of asking her not to reveal the experiences of other participants from past meetings—in particular one adoptee whom Marianne accused of "hounding" his birth mother. "Please speak only for yourself," Sam kept pleading.

Silently, I agreed with Sam. Marianne was out of line. Her voice became louder and louder, and then she abruptly began to sob and rail against her stepmother for making her give up her baby.

I spoke with Marianne on the phone a few days later. "Hope I didn't scare you the other night at Sam's," she said cheerily. I told her truthfully that she hadn't scared me at all. I didn't tell her that I had recoiled from her outburst. I was only sorry I could not feel an alliance with another birth mother.

A month later, Marianne called to tell me that she'd been told that one could petition the D.C. Superior Court to have adoption records opened. "I'll call them for you right now!" she offered.

"*I'll* call them, Marianne," I said, too firmly, perhaps. It was the last time we talked.

I called the court.

"You need a lawyer to do it," a clerk told me.

"I can't do it myself?"

"You could familiarize yourself with our laws, maybe read the books in a law library, and then maybe you could do it," she said.

"I heard there was just a form to fill out."

"Used to be. Not now."

"Are there any guidelines at all?"

"Used to be."

I hung up. I remembered Becca Dietz had given me the name of a genealogist in the Washington area named Sue who sometimes helped people with search problems. I found her number and called. Sue didn't search, but she was available for advice.

Sue was as measured and businesslike as Marianne was eager.

She asked me many questions. "Where was the adoption finalized?"

"I don't know."

"You may be able to get that information from Winnicott. It's critical. Otherwise why petition a court if you don't know it's the right court?"

"I thought I couldn't get anything from Winnicott."

"Sure you can! You can probably get any forms that you signed— your relinquishment, maybe other stuff. I'm pretty sure you can find out what court it went through."

We talked a little longer. She told me some horror stories about records that had been burned or otherwise destroyed. There were places where it was now virtually impossible to search, she said.

After we hung up, a part of me shut down. It was the same part that had not called Winnicott back, that had not read about adoptee searches in the seventies, that had tried to disappear. It was the part that felt there was no chance of success, so why make an effort that was doomed from the start? I couldn't bring myself to call Winnicott or ALMA. I couldn't bring myself to go back to Sam's. I hated his controlling ways, hated listening to the adoptees' complaints. I didn't know what to do next, so once again I did nothing.

Without a clue that I was simply suffering from profound discouragement, I again told myself—and Michelle, and my shrink, and Harvey—that I wasn't really searching, anyway, and I didn't want to be pushed. Nine months later, I received some information that, like the Soundex form letter, showed me one more time what my hidden feelings had been all along, but until it was drilled into me again and again that my feelings were just so tender I could not stand for them to be touched, I simply didn't get it. Again and again, I was able to suppress or ignore any glimmer of love for him. HIM. Whom? I didn't know who he was or who he would be. He was a stranger— how could I feel love for a person about whom I knew nothing?

How, in this case, could I not?

12

THERE IS an enormous amount of fantasy surrounding adoptions. As a birth mother, my fantasy was that my son would have a better life with his adoptive parents than he would have had with a sixteen-year-old mother whose psychological resources were nil, and whose familial and financial ones were nearly so. Over the years, nothing has changed my mind about his adoptive parents. To my mind, they are still wonderful people. On the other hand, I find to my discomfort that I am less inclined to ignore the fact that someone is an *adoptive* parent rather than a biological one. For years I never thought twice about it. Now, I know there is a difference. I just don't know what that difference is, what it means, or whether it matters.

A birth mother who had remained single recently told me that her child's adoptive parents hadn't understood him that well. She was a balanced, reliable person, and I felt sure she meant what she said. But her son was nearly twenty-five when she found him, and she had never reared a child from day to day and year to year. I found myself thinking: How much understanding is lost in the daily business of life, when you have to get the boots on and see that they still fit and scrub the jacket cuffs with Wisk before you throw the coat into the wash and put nametags on the underwear before it's taken to camp? I found it hard to imagine that adoptive parents committed more or worse errors per capita than the rest of us, even with the added psychological baggage adoptive families carry.

I had recently met an adoptive father at one of Sam Friedman's support-group meetings whom I had admired greatly. His daughter no longer wanted contact with him and his wife; she had found her birth mother, and though her mother was unstable and dysfunctional, the daughter wanted to live with her.

The adoptive father was in much the same kind of pain the rest of us feared—separation, rejection, loss. I felt very sorry for him, but I would have taken his problems more seriously if they did not seem so similar to those of many nonadoptive parents I know. The "child" was twenty; the "child" rebelled; the "child" wanted to distinguish herself. The father was thoughtful, responsible, and even humorous: it occured to me (but not, alas, to him) that he was the sort of father to whom a son or daughter inevitably returned, older and wiser and with a newfound appreciation for the father's forbearance and loyalty.

I was impressed by his bravery. Here he was, exposing his distress to a group that did not contain one other adoptive parent.

Before I began thinking about adoption and figuring out what effect giving up a child had on my life, I observed certain parenting behaviors with indifference or disinterested curiosity. Now I am riveted by almost everything an adoptive parent says or does, because I can't help thinking about my birth son, and how he was parented. The smallest gesture can assume a magnitude far beyond its true importance.

Laura made friends at the age of three with an adopted girl, and at one point her mother suddenly seemed nervous around me. I couldn't imagine why until I learned that she had just read my first book, in which I mentioned having a baby at sixteen and giving him up for adoption. For a while our encounters were strained.

I could not help remembering something this mother had said about her daughter one day at the playground, before she knew that

I was a birth mother but after I knew that her child was adopted. "Sure she's sweet as can be in public, but you know what we call her at home? 'The little bitch.' " I was so affronted I ran to the other side of the playground, where Laura was playing with her daughter.

Now I know them better, and I know that it was a joke. They love their daughter, and they would never call her names to her face. What made it personal to me in the first place was that I am the birth mother of a son who was illegitimate and therefore technically a bastard. It was agonizing to hear the feminine version of that expletive used on an adopted child. I might have grimaced hearing any parent jokingly call their daughter "the little bitch," but because their daughter was adopted I transposed their remark into the masculine and wondered if anyone had ever called my son "the little bastard."

As it happens, I respect these particular parents as much as any parents I know. I take their transgressions in stride, and I hope they do the same with mine. I do not think of the birth mother of their child with heartache every time I see them. I see these parents' cheerful involvement with every aspect of their daughter's life.

There are other adoptive families who will never be friends of mine, because each time I see them I feel absolutely terrible.

There is one mother I used to know slightly, from the neighborhood playground. She is small and dark; her daughter is big and blond. "My husband is tall," this woman told me when I first remarked on her daughter's beautiful size.

Then suddenly one day in the grocery store, there was a new baby.

"Oh!" I said, "I hadn't even noticed you were pregnant."

"I wasn't," she whispered. "They're adopted, but I don't make a big thing of it."

Then she whispered that the baby was actually the biological full sibling of her daughter.

I gasped. That a couple had given away two children! How had this come to pass?

My acquaintance shrugged. "It's a miracle," she smiled happily, misreading my gasp of horror as one of surprise. "We were so lucky."

I know that it happens. I even knew from the "Baby Hunt" article that some couples give away child after child, but I can not contain my discomfort at the thought. It astonishes me now, when there is no stigma at all to buying a condom in the drugstore or, better yet, getting an IUD or a Norplant inserted at one of the no-guilt clinics run by respected organizations such as Planned Parenthood, that women are still copulating and conceiving and gestating and giving birth—and making adoption plans for their babies, one by one.

Nothing could have put me through the nightmare a second time. Was there no one—no doctor or counselor—who had told the birth parents that they had many options for preventing another pregnancy? I couldn't stand to think about it.

I realize there are pregnant women who feel that they are unprepared to be mothers but unwilling to have an abortion. They feel abortion is wrong. I can understand that feeling, and I would never try to impose my own, which is that it may be more wrong and in the end far more painful, both physically and psychologically, for both mother and baby, to carry a pregnancy to term and give away a child.

I believe there are climates of approval or disapproval that cloud or clear the moral weather of a time and place and make it possible or impossible to feel all right about certain actions, and that these climates affect us so pervasively that we honestly believe that we are making individual moral choices, while in reality we are simply responding to the zeitgeist. It is my conviction that in most cases it is the prevailing moral climate that makes real reproductive choice possible or impossible for a pregnant girl or woman. In "Baby Hunt," Dorothy Kalins wrote, "We buy a guide to colleges and choose places with the best adoption laws and strongest anti-abortion sentiment. That means Bible Belt states, where religion or economics would favor a girl carrying to term—ironic for a pro-choice couple."

I thought of a friend of mine who said, "Adoption would be a feminist issue if the feminists weren't doing the adopting."

Kalins reported that eighty percent of adoptions are achieved through ads these days. My friend Susan, the obstetrician, gets glossy packets from couples searching for a baby. One time a couple she had treated for infertility came to her with a pregnant teenage girl and said they wanted the girl to have the best prenatal care, for which they would pay. Susan told them, "I would be happy to treat this young woman and deliver her baby, but she will be my patient, and so the confidentiality laws mean that I will discuss her condition only with her. And because she is in a crisis situation, she must have counseling." Susan never saw the couple again.

I asked her why she did it.

"Peggy, I knew *you!*"

Her answer took me aback. "What did knowing *me* tell you?"

"Peggy!" She seemed incredulous. She spoke slowly, as if I were an idiot: "That it's something . . . you . . . never . . . get . . . over!"

Oh, that.

The adoptive father I met at Sam Friedman's had been to a recent conference on adoption, and he expressed embarrassment at the attitude of some younger adoptive parents. "It's all, HOW can we get a baby? How can we close the deal as fast as possible? When we adopted you went to an agency, and they really put you through the mill, and then you waited, sometimes for years, for a child who needed adopting. Nowadays, it looks ruthless."

I found as I learned more about adoption that there was some debate about the difference in social stature between birth parents, who are usually less educated and poorer, and adoptive parents, who are almost always at least middle class and comparatively well off. When birth mothers talk about coercion, they are not talking about the more obvious sorts that took place in the fifties and early sixties— parents dragging their daughters to homes for unwed mothers, where keeping one's baby was overtly discouraged—but of the subtle sorts of societal coercion.

My neighbor Barbara, who was so outraged at Robby DeBoer's fantasy that Baby Jessica was really her daughter, carried in another woman's womb, also spoke of adoption as a class issue, but at the time we talked I didn't know what she meant. Now, a couple of years later, I understand her point of view, and I realize that she is not the only nontriad member who sees adoption as potentially exploitative. Even some lawmakers recognize that a woman who is pregnant and feels she is unable to provide for her child may give up the baby for adoption out of self-contempt. A 1992 California adoption law spelled out that a woman considering making an adoption plan must be informed that the family she chooses to adopt her child "is not better than you are, just different." Reading "Baby Hunt," I was saddened by Kalins's description of the woman whose child she and her husband eventually adopted: She was "in many ways . . . every birth mother. A child of divorce, in her early twenties, never any money."

I have heard of adoptees who are relieved at having been brought up by economically secure parents. They felt saved from a life of poverty. I have also heard adoptees bitterly say that their mothers should have kept them no matter what, and that no amount of love and care could make up for their abandonment.

Abandonment. I hate that word. One birth mother said to me recently that we should just say it: Adoption is abandonment. That places it in perspective, she said, and maybe more people will see it as the choice-of-last-resort.

In the past adoption was practiced as "a service for children," in the words of the Child Welfare League of America, or CWLA. That is changing. The National Conference of Commissioners on Uniform State Laws, or NCCUSL, is an organization composed mostly of lawyers and judges who are appointed by the governor of each state to try to standardize certain state laws. Subcommittees of appointees work in various fields of law, such as commerce or labor or, in this case, adoption, collecting information and recommendations. Eventually the committee writes a proposed law that must be approved by NCCUSL as a whole before being sent to the states, where the recommended acts must be sponsored by a legislator before they can be voted on and passed into law in any particular state. When, in 1994, NCCUSL proposed a Uniform Adoption Act, the CWLA put out an eight-and-a-half-page analysis of the proposed law pointing out how it "focuses on the rights of adults to adopt children, with inadequate attention to fairness for all parties to an adoption, particularly birth parents and children." The CWLA's goals, by contrast, were to "ensure quality services which lead to sound adoptions for children with stable, nurturing adoptive families."

The CWLA's analysis pointed out that

The act appears to suggest that simply informing a birth parent that personal and legal counseling are available satisfies any legal requirement. This minimalist approach is particularly troubling in light of the fact that many adoptions that end up in the courts and media involve birth mothers and birth fathers who did not receive any professional counseling to arrive at the best plan available for themselves and their child. . . .

One of the most onerous sections of the entire act is the extremely limited time a parent has to revoke a consent or relinquishment: '192 hours (8 days) after the birth of the minor' [Section 2-404(a)]. It is safe to assume that most, if not all, women are still recovering physically eight days after giving birth. This extremely limited time frame fails to:

–allow for complications related to delivery, medications administered, c-section deliveries, or other frequent complications related to child birth;

–take into account that many women are struggling emotionally with the adjustment to having given birth to a child, even under the happiest of circumstances;

–take into account that women who have experienced an unplanned pregnancy often go through extensive periods of denial and fear, in which their ability to plan realistically for their child's future is dramatically impaired; and

–take into account that many of these mothers are also struggling with relationships with the birth fathers and with their own parents and other family members.

Application of the eight day time period illustrates its inherent unfairness in light of the realities of labor and childbirth. If a woman signs a consent 6 days after giving birth, for example, she has two days to change her mind. If she signs a consent after her infant is 8 days old, her consent is irrevocable. Providing the mother with no time period for reconsideration under such circumstances seems arbitrary and inherently unfair. . . ."

This 8-day time period serves to expedite irrevocable consents by birth parents; it does not recognize or respect the rights of birth mothers. It clearly does not represent sound practice or quality services to children and families.

Further on in the CWLA's assessment is a paragraph headed "Records, Confidentiality and Access." The CWLA writes,

While the act does not expressly prohibit open adoption arrangements, the act primarily emphasizes sealed records and limiting access to information. . . . the focus of the act is on keeping the adoption 'closed' and all records of an adoption sealed for 99 years after the adopted individual's birth. Openness in adoption is a growing phenomenon, and most importantly, it has been shown to be in the best interests of children when utilized appropriately and in a manner that is sensitive to the needs, feelings, and capabilities of all members of the adoption triad. The act's omission in this regard is unacceptable.

As the Child Welfare League of America pointed out, "Virtually all of the key national organizations in the field of adoption—representing thousands of adoptive parents, birth parents, and adopted children and adults—have gone on record to oppose the proposed Uniform Adoption Act." These include the National Council of Juvenile and Family Court Judges, Catholic Charities USA, Adoptive Families of America, the American Adoption Congress, the North American Council on Adoptable Children, and the National Association of Social Workers.

Elizabeth Bartholet, the Harvard Law professor who referred to Baby Jessica as her birth father's "genetic product," is in favor of the act, as is the National Council for Adoption (NCFA), an umbrella organization for many agencies specializing in private adoptions. The NCFA was actively involved in drafting the proposed act.

In "Baby Hunt," Kalins described the ad she and her husband wrote, and then she reported her surprise that there were some newspapers that would not take the ad. The state of Georgia went so far as to outlaw ads by prospective adopters. To me, advertising for a mother to give up her child seemed like soliciting an unnatural act. To me, it is not natural—of nature—to give up a child. Kalins's phrasing, "You use the proper bait for the fish you hope to catch," made me flinch.

Kalins wrote of a conversation with a potential birth mother: "[My husband's] answers are typically straightforward and honest; I feel myself witholding, wanting to say the right thing." At another point she described talking to her lawyer on the telephone about a birth mother she had found whom she loved. The birth mother was taking classes at her local police academy. " 'Watch out,' he says when I mention police courses, as if too bright was no good."

At times, Kalins sounded arrogant: "She [a birth mother, on the telephone] asks us about discipline. It takes me a while to realize *she's* interviewing *us*."

I have a feeling that my birth son's parents, applying to Winnicott, were asked tougher questions than that one.

Kalins came across, to me, as a woman desperate to have a child. I knew that desperation, and I was sympathetic. I felt that the problem was not of rehabilitation but enlightenment: Kalins had never heard a conflicting point of view.

When Kalins referred to states with "good" adoption laws, she was referring to those with the shortest waiting period before adoptions became final. She avoided such states as California, where it took longer. I couldn't help feeling that Kalins might rethink her goals if she were told, by someone she knew and trusted, that although in California it took a long time for an adoption to become final, when it was final you could rest assured that the woman who gave up her child had done it of her own free will and that she had been given every opportunity to make another decision.

According to the 1992 California law, anyone considering placing a child through independent adoption must receive guidance from an advocate who may not have a fiduciary relationship with the person facilitating the adoption (usually, the lawyer for the adopters). The "family" considering placing a child for adoption, as California Bill 1148 puts it, must hear at four separate meetings how they may keep their child. Families must also receive this information in writing. The birth mother's consent is educated. She is informed that "a) Secondary infertility is common among birth mothers; b) The family you choose is not better than you are, just different; c) If you place your child you may search at a later date but your child may not be willing to have a reunion and, if they are willing, that reunion won't replace lost years; and d) The placing of your child for adoption will have lifelong implications for you and your family."

Birth parents in California are given full disclosure of identifying information about the prospective adoptive parents. The adoption is totally revocable, without a court hearing, for four months. The prospective adoptive parents may not leave the state without the birth family's permission for that four-month period. I couldn't help feeling that in California, adoptive parents know that the child they adopt is one whose mother *really* made an adoption plan, and that the child needs them, in order to have a family, every bit as much as they need that child.

There was a point Kalins described in her article when a birth mother whose expenses she and her husband had paid changed her mind at the last minute and kept her child. "On the eve of her delivery, despite . . . our constant attention, the battle is lost." I had to believe that it was her grief, her desperation, and her crushed hopes that wrote that line.

The year before Laura went to kindergarten I met a single mother at a private school where a friend of mine teaches. We had both applied to the school, and our daughters were interviewed in a group of prospective kindergarteners. Neither the other mother nor I had been able to leave the room where the kids were being observed. After the interview, we went to a coffee shop with the girls and talked about our problems with separation. She revealed that she had not yet—in one-and-a-half years—left the classroom at her daughter's pre-school. I was amazed that anyone could be worse than I was. She said her daughter absolutely couldn't *bear* for her to go out of the room.

"Were you that way as a child?" I asked, thinking of a friend whose daughter was in Laura's preschool class at the YMCA. Every morning the little girl cried in the teacher's arms when her mother left, and the mother told me she herself had wanted to stay home with her own mother until she was—oh, in law school. Recognizing her childhood feelings in her daughter (and remembering that she herself had been a successful student in spite of them) had enabled my friend to confidently reassure her daughter and to separate. Day after day.

"She's adopted," the mother answered, impatiently I thought.

"Did you know the birth parents?" I was still trying to find the key in heredity. Wrong tack.

The mother glared at me. "Yes, but I hardly think this is an appropriate time to discuss it," she whispered harshly.

Since that day I've heard a lot of unhappy adoptees talk about the primal wound of being separated from their biological mothers at or soon after birth. I know that such trauma can be serious, but when I see a mother talking about how her adopted daughter cannot bear to have her leave the room I do not immediately blame the primal wound. My first thought is that the mother is like me. She has a reason, rational or not, to believe that she should not turn her back on her child for an instant. In other words, that there is work to be done there.

"Adoptive parents have a particular problem in accepting the developing independence of their . . . youngster. They tend to view any disengagement from themselves and an attachment to others as an abandonment and a return to the lonely insecure feelings associated with the parents' preadoption childless period," wrote the authors of *The Adoption Triangle*. "[Adoptive parents] tend to be overprotective of their children. . . . [They] also tend to overreact to illnesses in their children, as if they fear that something will happen to take them away from them."

In the margin I noted, "So, I am an adoptive parent." None of this is easy.

13

Once undertaken, the process of search is so distressing that years may pass between the first request for a birth certificate and the final telephone call to the birth mother. Each new revelation must be absorbed by the adoptee and reconciled with his daily life before the next step in the search can be undertaken.

Linda Cannon Burgess, *The Art of Adoption*

EVERY MONDAY MORNING I would tell myself, This evening I'll go to a Contact meeting, but by early afternoon, when I had failed to call Harvey to ask him to come home early to babysit Laura, I would know that I was avoiding it again. I made the excuse that it was hard for me to get out of the house in the evening. I was still leading a support group with the Alliance for the Mentally Ill, and although that was only one night a month, it seemed to be all I could handle.

There were small irritations that also kept me away from the meetings, although I tried to remind myself that they were, really, negligible. The modest fee bothered me, since I was on a strict budget and reserved ten-dollar extravagances for Polly Pockets and Barbie accoutrements. But what troubled me most about the meetings, I think, were the adoptees. The adoptees at the meetings were mostly very young, and I hope I would be the last person to criticize them for their self-centeredness or their anger, but I didn't feel I wanted to be in the room with them just now. I needed to find a different kind of group, with members whose self-centeredness and anger more closely approximated my own.

During the spring of 1994 I had begun writing in earnest, and by June I had finished a lengthy book proposal.

Two weeks later, Laura graduated from nursery school at the YMCA. I kept reminding her that in the fall she would go to kindergarten at the school up the street that had a playground she already liked. She never answered, or even looked at me, until finally, on her last day at the Y, she said, "I can't figure out why you're not worried."

"Worried about what?" I asked.

"About never seeing this place again," she said.

"Oh, Sweetheart, we'll miss it, but we can always come back and visit. I thought *you* weren't worried."

"Well, I *am*," she said.

I told her that we could come back to the YMCA in the fall and tell her teachers all about kindergarten.

"Good," she said, and that seemed to be the end of it.

The next day we drove upstate for the summer. As I looked back on my year-and-a-half of waffling and uncertainty about my search and about writing about my memories, I finally felt ready to begin— I *had* begun—but I still couldn't figure out how I would explain the story to Laura someday. In the course of negotiating the contract with my publisher, I drove back into the city to talk with my editor and others. At one point I was asked to confirm that I would be available for publicity.

"Of course," I assured them. "Naturally."

Of course I would be delighted to go on stage and screen to talk about how it was, being pregnant in the pre-*Roe v. Wade* era. How it was, keeping a dark secret. How it was, wondering about a "baby" for thirty years afterward. How it was, telling my second child, who thinks she's my only child, about the first child, who isn't a child any longer and whom she may never meet anyway.

No problem.

When I received the contract, I immediately called Michelle and told her I couldn't do the book.

"Oh, don't be *ridiculous,* Laura won't be four forever," Michelle said. "When it's time to tell her, you'll point to some darling teenager on the street and say, '*That's* how young I was, *very* young—*much* too young to be anybody's mommy.' Laura isn't you and me, you know. She's much more sanguine about all this kind of stuff."

Now, there was a thought that hadn't occurred to me, but it had a lovely ring to it. "She is?" I committed Michelle's script to memory—it would do for starters, when I needed to start—and went ahead on this book.

The steps in my search extended in different directions, like the spokes of a wheel—not in a straight line, one by one, like the rungs of a ladder. I called Iowa, then Maryland, then New York. I went to a meeting, then read another book, then rested. Telephone call, letter, meeting, book: They were all shifting the weight away from the hub of me and my memories, out toward a wider arc of knowledge.

One day, realizing that I'd been troubled by the recurring thought that there was a possibility Linda Cannon Burgess, the author of *The Art of Adoption,* which I had found so helpful, might have placed my son for adoption, I wrote to her.

When I finally sent off my letter to Burgess, I also sent her a copy of *My Sister's Keeper,* as a thank-you for her book. I also had a second reason for sending it: We had the same publisher, and I wanted to establish myself as an equal, of sorts.

Burgess wrote back immediately to say that she had not been with Winnicott in 1965. She advised me to go to Winnicott in person and ask them what they could do for me. She said she thought I probably wanted to know if my son had escaped my sister's illness. One rainy Tuesday I dialed Washington information and got the number of the Winnicott Foundation. I had drunk a cup of coffee, to fortify myself. I sat in my most comfortable chair. And then I made the call to Winnicott, to ask for their address. To my surprise, the person who answered was friendly, and she gave me a new name to write to. The woman who'd previously "dealt with" birth mothers apparently was no longer in charge of us.

I hung up and composed the letter that appears in the introduction to this book. As I wrote the letter, I realized that my sister's illness was a legitimate reason to worry about my son's health. He was now of an age when mental illness, if he was susceptible, would almost surely have manifested itself. I didn't think about it too much, though. I needed to get the letter out before I lost my nerve. Also, I wanted it to be crisp, to suggest (I hoped) that I knew my rights— even though I didn't, exactly. I tried to be polite while intimating that polite was not the only way I could be. Start from a position of strength.

Done.

Heartened, I called the hospital where I'd given birth and was given instructions for ordering a copy of my medical records.

Done.

Two letters were popped into envelopes, stamped and addressed, and cast upon the storm-tossed seas of the U. S. mails. I expected no answers.

At one of Sam Friedman's meetings, I'd tucked a blank subscription form into my pocket for a magazine called *Reunions*. The form included an offer for classified advertising at a reduced rate.

Sitting at the kitchen desk upstate, where I'd sat in the same lamplight the year before, writing a letter to Becca Dietz and a note to myself to call Contact, I composed an ad: "For a book, I would appreciate hearing from other birth parents about how relinquishing a child affected their parenting of subsequent children. Confidential." I wondered if other birth mothers had problems like the ones I'd had with Laura.

I mailed it in.

The ad came out in the autumn issue, the first copy of *Reunions* I had seen. It turned out to be mainly a magazine for planning family reunions: It offered articles on genealogical research as well as organizational details such as advertising, nametags, and cleanup-crew assignments. In the back pages, however, I found my ad under the heading "Adoption Miscellany." I didn't expect many answers, considering the probable readership of the magazine, but the dozen I received offered ample confirmation of my suspicions about my own neuroses. The first letter arrived almost immediately:

> Dear Ms. Moorman,
> I relinquished my son in 1975 when I was seventeen years old. I never was allowed to see my son, I was put under before he was born, never was offered the chance to see him in the hospital (I was put on a separate floor), and was afraid to ask. When the name bands were checked upon release from the hospital, when they brought him in and pulled his foot from the blanket, I absolutely lost it. The lawyer sent from New York to get my child (private adoption) was so rattled by my emotional state he ran and hid in the closet with my son. I clung to the memory of that bundle in his arms; the blanket had lions all over it.
> In 1987 I had a second son. . . . The pregnancy went fine and I was deliriously happy waiting for Jeff's birth.
> The day I went into labor I cried when they put me into the wheelchair and took me to labor and delivery. I didn't know why I was so nervous and upset, so I put it down to fear of the delivery. When Jeff was delivered, I felt so detached. . . . I told the doctors that my first child was killed in a car wreck at age two. I was so ashamed of giving a child up. . . .
> When we were leaving the hospital I was clutching him so hard. I just knew the nurses were going to stop me and take him. I was really relieved to get him home.
> Once we were settled I started thinking he was going to die on me. He had ear infections and was sick a lot with high fevers. I would sit by his crib at night and cry and pray he'd get better.
> I never left him with anyone besides his father, and even then I was a wreck until I got home. Basically the first year of his life was spent in our home. Needless to say, I was very overprotective and fearful of losing him. I even feared someone sneaking into our home and snatching him.
> When he was four I divorced his father and moved to Montana. I found myself terrified that my ex would abduct Jeff and even put the whole school on alert for his father. When my new husband raised his voice to Jeff I would get furious. Finally, after a year or so of this, I started letting go and allowing Claude to parent Jeff to a degree and allowing Jeff to run

around and play in our small, *safe* farming town. I feel we have
a healthy relationship now.

This year I searched for and located my first son, learned
his name, and got a photo of him from the library. I have made
no contact because his parents do not want me to. The changes
in me are phenomenal. I feel like a ton of bricks has been lifted
from my shoulders. Until I found him I had never considered
that his adoption had influenced my parenting methods with
Jeff. I wasn't able to 'protect' my first son, so I doubled up on
Jeff.

The one fear I haven't been able to conquer is the fear of
my dying and leaving Jeff alone. Since I've searched, this fear
has actually worsened. Hopefully when the emotions I'm feeling die down some this fear will lessen. I guess the only way I
would ever leave Jeff is through death, which in my mind
would be abandoning him just as I always felt I did [my first
son]. Although in both instances the abandonment would be
or was unwilling, it still is an abandonment, and I feel the
blame would be all mine.

Thanks for the opportunity to tell this. I hope you find it
useful.

Sincerely,
Jaymie F.

It took me a long time to answer Jaymie's letter, which I managed
to misplace the way I'd misplaced nearly every significant bit of paper
relating to birth mothers or adoption. Even if I hadn't put it into
the wrong file, though, I would have waited. Except for her initial
distancing of herself from her second child, in the hospital, our
stories seemed identical. When I finally found her letter and wrote to
her, I thanked her and told her that in writing my book I would
describe her experiences in only general terms and leave out her
name. By return mail, she sent me a brief letter giving me explicit
permission to use her name: "I feel that until we quit hiding ourselves
and our 'shame' we can't heal from our past. I am proud that I
have survived this nightmare and I absolutely refuse to hide another
second!" Jaymie offered to help me search; she had a background in
police work that might be helpful, she said.

I would have been satisfied with only Jaymie's letter, but there were others with similar stories. One birth mother wrote: "I became possessive and overprotective. Anyone who took extra interest in [my son] I immediately backed away from. This fear did not leave me until I found [my birthson]."

Or another:

> I found that I needed to be very close to my three children, as they were growing up and as adults. When they were children, I was very protective and tried to give them material things as well as so much love, as if to make up for the daughter I relinquished. All the while I was thinking of my daughter and wondering if she was taken care of. At times I thought no one could love her like me. . . . I don't think I would change anything in the way that I parented, because today I am very proud of my children, close to them, and we have a very nice relationship. They all grew up to be good people.

Some of the letters I received were heartbreaking. A woman in Florida wrote: "After relinquishing my daughter I made myself a promise I would never have another, and I never did. That is the way I punished myself. Never a day went by I didn't think of her. The problem is, you do bond with a baby before it is even born. I have always carried this around with me."

I found two birth mothers who were at peace with their decision. I was not surprised that both were women whose lives were permeated with religious faith. One, a Sufi, said that she had received "a ton of counseling." "I feel like I made that choice one hundred percent." When her daughter was eighteen, she had searched for her mother, who told me that the resemblance between the two of them was startling. "There's a Filipino saying, 'The child you try to hide is the one who will look just like you,' " she said, laughing. This birth mother had always felt that she had been a kind of conduit for the adoptive parents—a body through which their daughter had been made—much as Robby DeBoer had believed that Baby Jessica was somehow spiritually her daughter, even though she had been born to Cara Clausen. The Sufi birth mother felt closer to the adoptive mother than she did to her birth daughter, she said. "She's one of these warm southern women you could drop from a plane who'd make a friend on the way down."

I asked the Sufi birth mother if she ever had regrets.

"No," she said. "But if abortion had been available, I would have done it."

Another birth mother who wrote to me described herself definitively as a Christian. A writer and editor, she was the journalist and record-keeper for her extended clan. She also wrote articles on family traditions and holidays. She had done volunteer work over the years with pregnant girls, chauffeuring them to doctor appointments and teaching childbirth classes. "There is a definite theme here, if you've noticed: family." She had relinquished a baby in the mid-seventies and she wrote, "I never regretted that decision to carry to term, give life, and part from him. It was difficult, but it was a decision I have lived peaceably with. I put him in God's hands." She has been very close to her subsequent two children, even schooling them at home. "Was I thinking subconsciously, 'I had to let go of my first baby, but I won't let that happen again?' Was I trying to make up for that loss by overdoing it?" She felt comfortable with her own mothering style; at the same time, she was willing to examine its possible roots. It seemed to me that she had succeeded on a number of levels in learning from her experience and moving ahead in her life. I admired her; I hoped that her first child, too, was peaceful with her decision.

In September, Laura started kindergarten at a large public elementary school not far from our apartment. Four of her friends from the YMCA were going there, too. All summer long, she begged me to send her to the school two blocks from us, where an equal number of her nursery-school classmates were enrolled. I didn't know how to explain to her why I'd chosen the one I did. It was all done by gut feeling: The glamorous principal seemed tough and smart; the reading scores were much higher; there were plenty of gray-haired parents at the class picnics I'd ambled past in Riverside Park each spring. But I didn't know for certain that I was making the right choice, so I faked it, telling Laura that she was going to a wonderful school and that I knew it was the one where she would learn the most and be happiest.

When, toward the end of the summer, Laura's class assignment came in the mail, I called another YMCA parent, whose daughter was Laura's favorite friend from pre-K.

"K-122?" she said when I called. "But we're in K-109."

I called the other three families. All of their children were in K-109. Only Laura, of all her classmates, was in K-122.

I was sick. I called the guidance counselor. She spoke reassuringly—*very* reassuringly. "I personally would feel thrilled—and completely secure—if my own child had Laura's teacher for kindergarten," she said. "She's wonderful, in every way—loving, experienced, well organized. I mean that."

I knew her job was to make me feel better, and that I should perhaps add a measure of reasonable doubt to whatever relief I felt, but I was trying to be more confident about separating from Laura.

I said we'd try it.

"You're being very, very brave," said the guidance counselor.

The first day, Harvey and I walked Laura the six blocks to school. "Mommy, I want you to stay with me, and not just for a little while—for the whole day, every day, all year," Laura said calmly and clearly as we went inside and made our way through the crowd to her classroom.

Stepping in, I looked around, and so did Laura, and I could tell we were ticking off the same things: block area, house area, meeting rug, book corner, and, oh what *luck,* a fat orange guinea pig with a mild expression.

Then I noticed a slender woman with a shining halo of silver hair. Her eyes sparkled, their smile-lines permanently stroked upward. Whenever she bent down to greet a child she took a small hand gently in hers as she said hello. My arm shot up in a spontaneous gesture of triumph. "Yes!" I murmured, startling a father who was standing next to me.

I introduced Laura to her beautiful teacher. She pulled me down to whisper in my ear. "Do you remember how to pick me up after class is over?" she whispered. "Because maybe you'd better go."

Parents and babysitters were hanging around in a small play yard near the classroom. I stayed in the hallway outside Laura's room. Harvey told me later that the parents we had known at the YMCA had pulled him aside to ask, "How's Peggy doing? Is Peggy all right?"

"Peggy's doing well," Harvey assured them. "I really think she's going to be fine."

Every day I successfully resisted an urge to put aside "the unpleasantness," as I referred to this book. I was curious to know how life would change after I faced down some of my fears and memories. After writing about Sally and me, I'd never again felt the overwhelming, negative emotions that had dominated our sisterhood for decades. I hoped a new kind of peace was waiting for me this time.

Less than a week after I mailed my two missives—the ones to Winnicott and Fairfax Hospital—I was talking on the kitchen phone when the call-waiting signal began to beep. I tried to put my call on hold, but the phone just clicked, and I remembered I'd left the bedroom phone off the hook. I hung up, raced to the bedroom and picked up the receiver. "Don't hang up!" I said breathlessly.

"Oh!" said a pleasant female voice. "I thought I was getting an answering machine."

"Oh no," I said, huffing. "My answering machine works a lot smoother than this."

My caller laughed quickly, then switched to a more earnest tone to introduce herself. "This is Marjorie Lane at the Winnicott Foundation," she said, "and I'm calling to tell you how sorry I am that you never heard back from us before."

That was a good start. From my past experience and from what others had said to me about Winnicott, I could have dismissed this woman's manner, which although businesslike was also friendly. Instead I decided, cautiously, not to expect too much, but not to cynically write her off.

We talked for a few minutes. I asked her what she thought she could do for me, and I heard her rifling through papers.

"Why, he's nearly thirty!" she said of my son at one point. "I don't see why I couldn't contact him directly." She said she would send me a form that I could use to request parts of my file from 1965, and she said that I could waive my right to confidentiality.

A week later, I received a letter acknowledging mine, and the promised forms. I signed them, took them to my bank to be notarized, and sent them back to Winnicott. Marjorie Lane had seemed so eager to help me, I was sure I would hear more from her right away, but the days slipped by, and soon it was November.

I called her again. After all, it was possible that this time the mail really had been lost. I couldn't remember putting my letter, with the forms, in a mailbox, and I was possessed by the suspicion that I'd tossed it into a trash can or left it on a bus.

But it had arrived safely. Marjorie Lane apologized for her delay and said she would be sending me a packet soon. She sounded busy.

When it came, it consisted of a cover letter, a seven-page autobiography I wrote in 1964, and a copy of the document surrendering my son for adoption in which I gave up "forever any and all rights as parent of said child."

I fell upon the autobiography I had written for Winnicott when I was fifteen, but it was so sad and so unconsciously revealing that I quickly put it down as if it were too hot to touch. I read it a second time months later, so that I could quote from it here, but I did so reluctantly. In it, I sound determinedly, falsely chipper, though perhaps it would not seem so to anyone but the adult me. In loopy, hyper-legible script that screams "teenager," I waxed lyrical about my late father, my mother, and our cocker spaniel.

Here is my autobiography:

I've lived in Virginia all my life, in Falls Church and Arlington. My father built the house I live in now when I was 3. Daddy died on New Year's Eve last winter. I knew he was wonderful all my life; it's not something I realized suddenly.

I can't remember him ever being mad at me. I can remember scoldings, and times he drew the line about something, but he was never mad. He was very calm, and very smart. He could do everything, and fix anything. He was very artistic, and it was brought out in his photography, which he loved. He loved beautiful things and black walnut ice cream.

He had a personal integrity in everything he did. He was very honest, very polite, and my favorite father. He loved me, too.

Our house is pretty. It has high ceilings and lots of natural pine paneling and lots of wood. We have a nice yard and lots of trees. There's a big oak tree where Daddy made me a swing when I was little. I've always played outdoors alot. There's lots of woods near us, and there used to be a lot more. I've climbed a lot of trees, swung on a lot of grape vines, and fallen off a lot of bikes. We played in the creek and built dams and cities and had 'flash floods' and explorations to the far end of the creek, near the Potomac. I've been very lucky as far as friends + neighbors go, and about as far as anything else goes, too.

So lucky! I thought sarcastically, reading it thirty years later. To have a dead father and a mentally ill sister and a mother beaten down by despair. So lucky to have become pregnant at fifteen. What a lucky, lucky girl! It went on and on.

I went to a small elementary school, and a much larger Junior High. I've had good teachers almost every year with only a few exceptions. I enjoyed my first year of high school, and discovered I was interested in more than I thought. I made Advanced Placement English, which is an honor. I'm in a separate French class with people who've had French since 7th grade. I detest all math courses, but I found, to my surprise, I loved Biology.

My mother is very important in my autobiography. I'm very close to her, and I've always loved her very much. She's very funny sometimes, and my friends have always liked her, too. She's always given me more than my share of love.

We like the same things in people. She loves Dan almost as much as I, if possible. She's pretty . . . the most wonderful and bravest person in the world.

We have a brown cocker spaniel. He's fuzzy and loves Momma dearly but won't obey anyone. He would obey Daddy. His tail wags alot and he's very sneaky about taking things out from under peoples' noses.

I love to paint. I take art from John Bryans, a Washington artist. He's a realist and paints beautifully in water colors and oils. He's won many awards and is an excellent teacher. I won some awards last year in the school art show, a 1st and a 2nd place, and I sold an oil for $20.00. I was surprised and pleased.

I plan to go to college, somewhere near here or perhaps in Pennsylvania.

Dickinson appeals to me, but I don't know if I could get in.

Dan is a very wonderful person. His parents are very intelligent and understanding and he loves and respects them. [I describe Dan's siblings.] I love them, but Dan laughs and says I only see their good sides.

Dan's college boards scores hit in the 700s. He didn't make good grades last year, but he wasn't "inspired" and didn't work at it.

He's in the Navy for just 6 months. I think it's doing alot for him. He is more of an extrovert, and has more respect for authority and the opinions of others. He's working very hard in Boot Camp and has earned the respect of the drill instructor, as well as the recruits. He's very strong and has done excellently on physical tests and has also come out on top in intelligence tests. He's top candidate for Private First Class, has qualified for a special program. He's also figured out how to swipe Kool Aid from Heaven knows where.

He's very sensitive, and sometimes explosive when he feels he's been wronged. He's often shy, but sticks to what he believes and is virtually immovable when he makes up his mind about something.

He hopes to go on to college next year, and we do hope, still, to be married some day.

Lane's letter failed to touch on the purpose of my original request: whether or not she would find out for me if my son was all right. She had seemed so kind on the telephone, so willing, so reasonable about his age and mine and the fact that we were both adults. I surmised that she must have been new to the job, and that after hanging up with me she had probably been admonished by someone more experienced. How could I have been so naive, I wondered, as to believe that someone at Winnicott would help me? As if we were in a gangster movie, I thought: They got to her.

Four days later I received my records from Fairfax Hospital. The photocopied pages, printed on slick paper, are fuzzy and hard to read, but I could make out most of the notes about my condition and about the various medicines I was given. The final page was for the most part blurred beyond legibility. On the very last line, however, one short word can be deciphered: "baby"—. That brought me up short. I breathed deeply. I could feel tears welling up. I blinked them back.

Baby. The baby. Well, yes. Of course there was a baby. The baby was the whole point, once he was born, once he was a baby and not just the primary ingredient of a problem pregnancy.

There were surprises. The baby was delivered by low forceps. I didn't know that. And my condition, so fragile-feeling to me, consistently was declared "good" by nurses. "Some pain in episiotomy," the doctor wrote, as he noted my anemia and prescribed iron. Two days later he noted, "Episiotomy healing well. No complaints." It was my habit not to complain. (Now, I am making up for lost time.) On the twenty-fourth of January I had "no engorgement of breasts." (My mammary glands were waiting until the middle of the night on the twenty-seventh, when I would be in my childhood bed, scared to death at the swelling and the heat.) January 25. Discharged.

When Marianne told me that I could write for my records, she had said, "Wait'll you see what they gave you to keep you quiet!" I hadn't considered it that way, so I gave some thought to the notion of suppression, but I still felt that my situation didn't suggest that perspective. It is true that in the labor and delivery rooms I hadn't made a sound—not for a long time, at least—but other women had, and I was pretty sure no one would have stifled me. But I asked my friend Susan, the obstetrician, if she would look over the papers and tell me what she thought. I was curious about the medical aspects of the birth, since afterward I had felt like the baby at the center of Solomon's judgment on a day when his wisdom backfired.

Susan was visiting us in New York. I watched as she flipped through the pages. I held my breath. "It doesn't say. . . . Uh huh. . . . Well, it looks pretty normal. You had a good doctor. It's amazing how abbreviated the notes are by today's standards. Nope," she said, handing the pages back to me. "Nothing irregular."

"What about the episiotomy?"

"All the way into the anus. But that's what I would have done. Better than one that cuts to the side, I think. He was a good doctor."

What had I expected? For Susan to pat me on the arm and say, God, what you *went* through? Probably. But what had I gone through? Nothing out of the ordinary: just what most women go through to make a baby. No big deal, I guess, unless you have nothing to show for it, in the end. I suppose that was the point, in my case: having nothing that showed.

The biggest surprise was the baby's weight at birth: *eight* pounds, six ounces. Why would I have remembered seven-six all these years? I distinctly recall my mother saying "seven pounds, six ounces" to me, as I lay in the hospital bed, wondering why my abdomen was still large. There it was, in gray and white. Eight pounds, six ounces. No wonder the doctor had to tug him out. There was no number marked where the form called for "length," but I have a feeling this kid was long (that the man he is now is tall). His father was six feet. My father was six feet. The baby had to have had frame enough at birth to support all those pounds and ounces. I wondered if he took after Dan. I wondered if it would bother me, if we met, if he did.

But then I remembered that I weighed eight pounds, eleven ounces at birth, and I am only five-foot-six. I wondered if he took after me. I wondered if it would be painful to discover that, if we met. If, if, if, if, if, if, if.

I waited, but Marjorie Lane did not call. I felt like a fool.

I needed to talk to someone. I was busy—it was early December and Hanukkah was here and soon it would be Christmas—but I was constantly aware of waiting. I hated waiting; finally I decided it was time to stop. Leafing through the messy notebook in which I'd begun jotting various names, I came up with a number for a group in New Jersey, "Origins," that was specifically for birth mothers.

Mary Anne Cohen answered the telephone. I told her my story and she asked if I was searching.

I wanted to be honest. "I'm not sure," I said. I talked about Laura, and how even though I was writing a memoir of my experience, I dreaded the day I would have to tell her about it. Mary Anne listened quietly. "I'll send you some stuff about that," she said. I could tell it was something she'd heard many times before.

We talked a little longer. I said that I was curious to know if overprotectiveness of subsequent children was common among birth mothers. "Oh, some overprotect and some hold themselves back," she answered. "It's usually one or the other."

Two newsletters soon appeared in my mail, along with a booklet titled "Secret-Sharing With Loved Ones: Personal Stories of Telling Children and Others." On the first page, I found a statement of the group's policy regarding search help: first, the birth mother must be "out of the closet." "That is, she must have shared the fact that she gave up a child with her immediate family, husband, other children, her parents, and the birth father, if he did not know at the time." Second, the birth mother must be prepared to do "what is best for the child, whether that is waiting for years for a direct contact, or, in the case of a rejected child, taking the child back into her home with open arms.

"We do not encourage search for idle curiosity. Our goal for each of you is reconciliation."

As far as I knew, I was trying to find out that he was all right. Was that "idle curiosity?" Certainly my paralysis made my curiosity idle, for I was again unable to go forward at all. I had made a leap, communicating with Winnicott and ordering my hospital files, but the leap had led nowhere.

Once again I didn't feel good about any of it—my history, my not-quite-search, my writing—for I was still not at all ready to tell Laura. *They have their nerve,* I thought, as I read through the personal stories of a half-dozen women, none of whom seemed at all like me. Most of them did not have children who were a quarter-of-a-century younger than their firstborns, for one thing. And the children for whom they were searching were not thirty years old. The birth mothers who wrote of telling their other children about relinquished siblings also wrote about doing things that made me cringe, such as going to sports events and anonymously sitting next to their relinquished child and his family. I wouldn't call it stalking, and I could imagine the love that engendered the desire simply to be near a lost child, but it seemed . . . definitely not quite right, to me. Having grown up in a family where secrets and their consequent shame were part of the everyday mix, such skulking looked unhealthy, at best. At worst, it gave me the creeps.

I'm afraid I dwelt on whatever I found that seemed negative to me, and not on such articles as "Telling Your Other Children," which turned out to be very helpful. I didn't find that out until many months later, when I picked up the booklet again. "It is important to realize that while your children will probably be interested in their lost sibling, and ask many questions, they will never have the intensity of feelings, especially painful feelings, that you have, because they did not experience what you did: the birth, surrender, and years of secret guilt," Cohen wrote. She also noted that "if a child is too young to understand," she seems to "put away" the knowledge until a later time, when she is "mature enough to make some sense of it." It occurred to me that, as an immature birth mother, I had similarly "put away" the information in this article.

In another newsletter, there was an article about a judge in New Jersey, Alan B. Handler, who, in terminating the visitation rights of a birth mother in an informally arranged open adoption, said that the birth mother "intentionally abandoned" her child. "Because intentional abandonment involves the willful repudiation of parental obligations, a reversal of abandonment must, minimally, involve conduct that is tantamount to the purposeful resumption of parental obligation. At no time did she express the wish to undertake the normal parental responsibilities for the child. . . . Her interest was only in seeing the child and in being informed of his progress."

Only! Whenever I read such arguments, I wanted to go to sleep and forget I ever heard of adoption. I felt there was nothing I could say that could alter the point of view that would lead a person to such an unempathetic interpretation of the law and of one young woman's actions.

Luckily another judge, Daniel O'Hern, was, unlike me, fully awake and able to argue: "Is she [the birth mother] to be condemned because she sought, without full knowledge of the law, to provide a better place for her child to grow up?" he asked. "All we have is a confused and hesitant young woman. Recognizing her own weak-nesses . . . the birth mother . . . was willing to yield custody of her child to . . . the adopting parents, but did not want to give up all contact with her child."

Mirah Riben, author of both the article on this case and of a book called *The Dark Side of Adoption,* noted, "The word 'abandon' appears to be a legal term which is bandied about after the fact. We see it in this case, as we saw it in the case of Michelle Launders, mother of Lisa Steinberg." A judge ruled that Launders could not sue Joel Steinberg, her birth daughter's illegal adoptive father and the one who killed her, because Launders had "abandoned" her daughter when she gave her up for adoption. "Strange, isn't it, that before the fact agencies don't even like the words 'surrender' or 'relinquish,' but prefer instead to soften the blow by saying that birth mothers 'make an adoption plan.' Yet, in reality, what a birth mother is obviously doing according to the law is abandoning her child. One wonders how many birth mothers would go through with the process if they were being asked if they were willingly choosing to abandon their child."

In my relinquishment papers for the District of Columbia, I swore that I released "custody, guardianship and parental rights to said minor child to the Winnicott Foundation, a licensed charitable corporation . . ." and that I consented to "the adoption of said child by any person or persons that may be selected by the Winnicott Foundation without further consent" and "without notice." That I "desired the same to be done, believing that the best interests and welfare of said child will thereby be promoted;" and that I "fully" realized that I relinquished "forever any and all rights as parent of said child."

That is how one legally abandons a child.

At the end of the newsletter, I found a list of groups. One read, "Manhattan Birthparents Group. For details contact Joyce Bahr."

I called and left a message.

That afternoon, returning with Laura from the playground, I found a message from Joyce on my answering machine. I wrote down her number and lost it. I could have looked it up again in the newsletter, but I didn't.

I was going back over emotional territory that made me relive the sadnesses of my childhood, and it made me ache for an element in my own life that for lack of a better word could be called mothering. It's embarrassing to me, at my age, to admit it. But as the fall months blew by, I felt increasingly alone. I was particularly disappointed that I had not found a single birth mother with whom I felt comfortable. My experience with the Alliance for the Mentally Ill had been very different. Right from the start I felt at home with the other brothers and sisters of people with mental illness. There was an ease for me, with them, that I couldn't seem to duplicate with the women—admittedly a smaller number than I'd hoped for—with whom I'd been looking for birthmom sisterhood.

One day I picked up the phone and called Joyce Bahr again, the leader of the Manhattan Birthparents Group. Why hadn't I pursued this connection before? The answer to all such questions was, I am sure: Because I was afraid it wouldn't work out.

When Joyce answered the telephone, I introduced myself and then told her just where I stood. Where I *thought* I stood.

"I am not like Carol Schaefer (the author of *The Other Mother*)," I said defensively. "I haven't been thinking of my beloved son for thirty years and yearning for him all that time. I don't have the feeling, He's my child and I need to bond with him. My interest is in resolving my own miserable past. To begin with I wanted to figure out how to allow my daughter to separate from me without freaking out. Oh, and I'm not ready to tell her about her half-brother. I don't even know he's alive. And even though I'm writing a book about all this, I'm not ready to come out of the closet as a birth mother and I don't think I'm going to be ready until I'm forced to be."

Joyce listened.

"So if my motives aren't acceptable, I don't want to waste my time coming to a group where people are going to talk about giving a 'gift' to my son—my son who isn't registered anywhere and has never contacted his adoption agency—or who say I have to tell my little girl about her phantom brother before they'll give me any search help."

Joyce listened.

"I really want to find someplace where I can meet other birth mothers, but I don't want to have to toe some party line."

Joyce spoke. She had a slow voice ("Very Zen," I told Harvey) and spoke carefully and thoughtfully. "It sounds like you're dealing with issues of shame," she said. "I have a film and some other material that I could give you."

Joyce was the answer to my prayers. Her experience was not like mine—she had felt forced to relinquish her son; she had waited only the minimum number of years to search for him. She had found him and they had established a mutually loving relationship that was positive for his adoptive parents as well. Joyce stayed at his parents' house when she visited him. Joyce had become an advocate long ago. She petitioned the legislature, edited a newsletter, marched for open records. As she told me, "After I came out of the closet I couldn't shut up."

December 16, 1994

My conversation with Joyce Bahr was the turning point. I was heartened by Joyce's calm understanding and by her complete acceptance of me. I had finally met the mother I needed, and she was us, to paraphrase Pogo. She was a birth mother who, I knew, could help me find my way. As soon as I hung up the phone, I called the D.C. adoption court and asked again how to petition to open my file. Again, I was told there was no way to do it myself.

Then I called the woman in Maryland, Sue, to whom I'd spoken in the spring. When I called her this time and started to re-introduce myself, she interrupted me, saying, "Winnicott, right? January 15, 1965?" She had taken notes.

I told her I'd heard from Winnicott but that I wasn't positive my son had been adopted in Washington. She said I needed to call

Winnicott again to find that out. We talked a little about professional searchers. I asked if she knew any, and she said yes, but she could not give me their names. "Spend some time in a birth mothers' group, and sooner or later someone will give you the information you need," she said. "No one's going to give it out until they know for certain you're legitimate." She confirmed what I'd heard: The fee for a clandestine search was two thousand dollars.

When I dialed Winnicott later that morning, I asked for Marjorie Lane. Instead of simply asking my question about court jurisdiction, I blurted out my disappointment to her. I told her what I had thought—that someone there had prevented her from helping me.

"I'm not as new here as you think," she answered. "I'm just new in this job." As soon as she spoke, I was sorry I had allowed my suspicions to fester, for this woman was not against me, I could tell. She gave me the impression, this time, of someone with too much on her plate. She seemed distracted, overworked—not reticent. "Oh, I'm sorry," she said. "He *was* adopted in D.C."

"When we first spoke," I reminded her, "you said you might be able to contact him for me. Can you still do that? I mean, I don't even know if he's *alive,* and I would like some peace of mind."

"Oh I'm sure—at least I'm as sure as I can be—that he's alive and well," she said. "If anything had happened to him I know we would have heard."

"Why would you have heard?"

"Well, there are some families who are just part of the Winnicott community, and I feel sure we would know if something went wrong. Anyway, let me see what I can do. Perhaps I can send a letter to him in care of his parents. I doubt at his age that he's still living at home. Let's hope not, anyway."

Alive and well. Alive and well.

I looked at the window next to my desk and thought of throwing it open and screaming up and down the street: "He's ALIVE! He's ALIVE!"

Why did I think he might not be? Because I thought he might take after me or after my sister, I guess. I thought he might have inherited the depressive gene, the sorrowful gene, that threads through the Moorman side of his genetic makeup. I can't quite say that I thought he might have killed himself, but I had heard of two birth mother searches that had ended with that terrible news. I also worried he might have fallen out of a tree and broken his neck—the same thing parents usually worry about. Hit by a car on his bike. Drowned in the undertow at Rehoboth Beach. I don't know what I thought. But when I heard the words "alive and well" a sudden transfer of blood to my heart made me feel faint.

I didn't call Harvey because I wanted to tell him in person. I didn't call my psychiatrist because I would see her the next day. I didn't tell anyone because I didn't know whom to tell. When I picked up Laura at school that afternoon, I swept her into my arms. He's ALIVE, my darling, I didn't say. In my mind the words formed their own Möbius strip, turning endlessly upon themselves. he's alive he's alive he's alive he's alive . . .

I immediately wrote to Marjorie Lane—"I wonder if you can imagine how ecstatic (and how unglued) I feel after hearing you say that you're pretty sure my son is alive and well"—and sent her a copy of the children's book I had written and illustrated that was just out from Scholastic. I was proud of it, and also I thought it made me look successful. I considered sending a copy of *My Sister's Keeper,* but I decided not to. For one thing, I couldn't remember if Lane had said she would contact my son or his parents. In the end Lane did not send anyone anything.

After we had hung up, I had been so addled that all I remembered clearly were my final words, hurriedly called into the phone after we said a cordial goodbye: "I'll be holding my breath until I hear from you!"

By evening I was covered with hives. When Harvey walked in the door I told him what had happened before he had a chance to take off his coat. By nine-thirty, there were welts up and down my back, between my fingers, on my toes, on my abdomen, up the back of my neck. At five the next morning I was still wide-eyed and sleepless, but the hives were subsiding. I slept between six and seven.

I made breakfast, helped Laura dress, and packed her lunchbox. Harvey took her to school, and I went back to bed and set the alarm for fifteen minutes before pickup time.

The following Monday I went to my first meeting at Joyce's. There were only five of us in her living room, but it was a good group. We talked, offered one another advice, asked questions, and generally cross-talked our way through the evening.

Joyce spoke about the difference between sons and daughters, and how it was much more common for a daughter to search and much more likely that she would empathize with her birth mother. "When I was marching for open records," Joyce said, "more than one young man came up to our group and said, 'My mother gave me away; she rejected me. Why would I try to find her?' " Joyce had also encountered young male adoptees who said, "My mother has a right to her privacy." They all seemed to have a reason not to search. I hoped my son was in the second group. Of course there was a third group: those who never thought of searching at all. It was impossible to unravel the reasons for that. From my own experience, though, I knew that it was possible to make all sorts of excuses. Or a person might be so well-adjusted and busy he would feel no need to make the genetic connection.

I could hardly wait to recount my good news to the group, but after my turn there was an uncomfortable silence. It occurred to me in a flash that I didn't really *know* that my son was alive and well. I didn't really know anything at all.

Waiting. Waiting. Not a day went by that I did not wake up wondering if I might get a call from Winnicott. Even the fun of Christmas and Hanukkah with Laura couldn't erase the thought from my mind.

On New Year's Eve, Harvey and I watched the fireworks over Central Park, more beautiful than ever this year, and shared a bottle of champagne. It was a sweet, harmonious evening, and I felt fortunate, to have him and Laura and a fluted glass of elixir, but after a midnight kiss, I heard a thought creep into my mind. I tried to close it out before it became entirely conscious, but there it was. Thirty-one years ago on this night my father died; thirty years ago I was pregnant, less than a month away from delivery.

I waited out the holidays, expecting nothing. I have had a lot of jobs in my life, and I don't remember working much in late December, so I assumed that Marjorie Lane was similarly out of gear. I waited out January 3, Tuesday, the beginning of the post-holiday work week, and on Wednesday I called Marjorie Lane. The secretary asked who was calling, took down my name, left the phone, and then informed me that Marjorie Lane was in a meeting. That afternoon, she was "unavailable," and the following morning she was also "unavailable." She was only unavailable after I gave my name, in response to the question, "May I tell her who's calling?" I began plotting to give a fictitious one the next time I called. How could I disguise my voice? Why was she avoiding me?

I think she was avoiding me because she was overworked and hadn't had a chance to attend to my case. I found her unavailability disturbing and discouraging, and for a few days I didn't call, but then, on the eighth, I reached her. She sounded pleased to talk to me and said that on the sixth she had sent a letter to him in care of his parents, saying something to the effect that birth parents called Winnicott from time to time, and that I had shown consistent interest in his progress over the years. Could he send updated information for their files?

It was less direct than anything I would have sent, but then, I wasn't the sender. It was more casual than anything I could have composed, but perhaps cooler was better. I thanked her and felt relieved.

My relief lasted about half a day. I began to worry. How would we know the letter had reached him? How would we know that his parents would forward it?

I decided to wait until the end of the month and then ask Marjorie Lane to check.

14

If you want to discover your true opinion of anybody, observe the impression made on you by the first sight of a letter from him.

Arthur Schopenhauer

January 15, 1995

TODAY WAS MONDAY, never an easy day.

I've had a lot of trouble lately with anything involving documents, organization, deadlines, or short-term memory. For example, my keys. The building superintendent now keeps a set of mine by his front door, instead of in the box with the other tenants'.

Last week I hit a kind of nadir of forgetfulness. My friend Sydney called one morning. She needed to pick up various items her daughters had left at our apartment the previous afternoon, when they were playing with Laura.

"I'm here," I said.

"Are you sure it's convenient?"

"Positive, Sydney. Come ahead. I'm working. I'll be here until two-thirty."

She said she'd be right over, and we hung up.

As I stretched my arm to replace the receiver in the cradle, I noticed a packet I'd meant to mail the week before. I reached for it and tucked it under my arm. I walked to the living room, grabbed my coat, and left for the post office.

When I got downstairs, there was Sydney, pressing the buzzer for our apartment and looking dismayed.

Oops.

I told the story to a mother at school who is a neurologist. "There is a word for your problem," she said.

"There is?"

"Yes. *Stress.*"

If stress was the cause of my difficulties, then it was worsening, because the past week was a knot of forgotten obligations.

I slept through the afternoon. I had felt low all day, and toward evening my mood slipped another notch. I was inexplicably sad. I felt strange—just strange—but I couldn't say how, exactly. Harvey offered to make dinner, but I wasn't hungry. "I think I'm coming down with something," I told him. "I'm probably going to conk out when Laura does."

Laura seemed tired, too. That morning, when I'd taken her to school, she had started to whimper and whine when the bell rang for parents to leave and class to begin. "She's a little puppy," her teacher, Julie, remarked sympathetically, listening to Laura's unhappy sounds. That appealed to Laura, who began to whimper in truly canine fashion, with a few dramatic, slobbery snuffles thrown in.

"I have to go, Sweet Darling," I whispered to her.

The puppy whined loudly, but then, amazingly, it also spoke in English: "Give me to Julie."

"Julie," I said, "May I give this little puppy to you?"

"I would *love* a little puppy like that one," Julie said. Laura threw me a lick and I left.

At bedtime, as I opened an animal book Laura had brought home from school, I stroked her on the head. "Nice puppy," I said.

One of our cats was sitting on my lap, and Laura began to scratch its neck. "You big, handsome cat," she cooed. "You sweetie kitty."

Suddenly I thought I was going to cry. And just as suddenly, I remembered something.

"Laura, is today January 15?"

"You *always* ask me the date and I *never* remember what it is," Laura said.

I didn't have to look at a calendar. Every cell in my body told me today was January 15. Today my son turned thirty.

I put my arm around Laura. "Have I told you lately how much I love you?" I asked her. She smiled.

Laura went to sleep. I went back to the living room, where Harvey was reading the paper. I told him what day it was. "Oh, *sweetie,*" he said.

"Harvey?"

"What."

"Thank you for the daughter."

I was no longer tired, though I was still sad. I shook my head, thinking about the subconscious. I couldn't help remembering the day thirty years earlier, the dark day, the second hardest day of my life up to then. I wondered who was celebrating its anniversary tonight, whether there was a party, who was invited. *Happy birthday,* I beamed into the ether, hoping that he would somehow receive intimations of my warm wishes.

Then the intermittent bitterness I'd felt over the past year and a half, starting just after finding that my son wasn't registered with Soundex, overcame me with embarrassing force. I hated this feeling, but I couldn't deny it. I was bitter and I was angry, and that's what I was.

I realized I had been on tenterhooks since fall, when I first wrote to Winnicott. I now had an inkling of the anger that I had heard adoptees express. I was angry today, and not for the first time. I reminded myself that it was possible he did not even know that I was waiting to find out how he was. I tried to avoid the thought that he might not care that I was waiting.

My mind began to churn. The letter from Winnicott had gone to his parents on January 6. Presumably they did one of two things with it: They read it and threw it away, or they forwarded it to him. Either way, they must have known, or he must have, that I longed for a little word.

Did his parents have any idea what it had been like for me, producing that son for them, that first child of theirs—and of mine? Did their son have any idea that the fifteenth of January was a birthday for me as well? I thought, Can't they imagine what it is like for me on this anniversary? Can't they guess how I feel, wondering if I'll ever hear a word about him or from him? Do they have the empathy for that? Does he?

Then I thought, they could be away for the winter. How old are they? Retirees often do go away to a warm climate.

Maybe they haven't received the letter yet.

Maybe the letter was lost in the mail.

I expended a good deal of energy trying to figure out how he might feel: Maybe he resents being asked only for updated information, I thought, if he is secretly interested in a reunion. Maybe he's thinking, She gave me up and now she wants reassurance that she did the right thing. Or, She wants to know about me so she can decide whether or not to try to meet me. Or even, Why is she trying to rock the boat, after all these years? Or, Has she got her act together or is she a mess and hoping I'll support her? Of course, it is possible that because he carries my genes he may have been thinking, Where the hell did I put that letter?

Even if he got it and has it, when I consider the thirty-year-old men I have known, I remember that they were often uncomfortable with emotional issues. Maybe he can't figure out how to answer because this is an emotional issue for him.

I thought, Tomorrow he will be over thirty. I remember when people said, Never trust anyone over thirty. But *I* couldn't be trusted until I *was* over thirty. What kind of thirty-year-old is he?

The waiting became too much for me. One day a week or so later I simply woke up and realized I was sick of thinking about it. Like the many hiatuses in my search, this one felt like a final resolution: I had had enough; it was ruining my days; I was done, done, done. Obtuse as ever, I put everything away one more time—for the last time, as I always thought. I would never learn that each disappointment caused me to proclaim *finit,* dust off my hands, and congratulate myself again for putting it all behind me.

I told myself that it was no longer necessary to "deal with" the memory of my lost child. I had felt compelled to sift through the dust, if only to look for ways to improve my chances of making an independent daughter. I had needed to figure out how to stop worrying whenever Laura was out of my sight. There had been work to do, yes. I think I've done it, I now said to myself.

Laura now would go without me to her friends' houses to play after school. We would wave goodbye. She would take another grownup's hand. She would march down a city sidewalk, and I would go the other way, and until I picked her up at the end of the afternoon, I went in peace, to shop for groceries or pay my bills or take the cat to the veterinarian. I no longer sat by the phone, or counted the minutes, or arrived at the friend's house early, with some excuse. A year ago, I would have been as unready for these separations as she was.

Laura herself had the idea that cutting loose was part of her future. "When I'm seven or eight," she said angrily one day, after I'd said no to something, "it's going to be 'Alright, already' to *you,* Mom."

When Laura was two and stricken with constant ear infections, she never seemed to sleep. Once, having dinner with our friends Andy and Sique, I apologized for yawning and told them how tough it was. "Laura woke up six times last night," I lamented. "I get out of bed, get her out of her crib, rock her with her head raised so the ears will stop hurting, give her some Tylenol, put her down, and go back to bed. An hour later, she's crying again."

"She knows you need the attention," Sique said, patting my arm and smiling.

Now Laura was past the ear-infection business. She would still wake up in the night, but only once. She would climb out of her bed and find her way to me and burrow in beside me for the duration. I felt proud of both of us: Laura, that she got up alone in the dark to pad quietly from room to room, and me, that I needed her attention only once during the long stretch between bedtime and morning.

What did I need with further introspection? What did I need

with the real son, the loss of whom had triggered so many fears in me? I had Laura, we were doing fine, and that was that.

Naturally I couldn't bear it, so I wrote to Marjorie Lane.

> Dear Marjorie Lane: February 1, 1995
>   I realize you must not have heard from anyone in response to the letter you sent out on January 6, or else I would have heard from you. Do you think it would be a mistake to telephone and find out if the letter made it through the mails? I've kept myself busy thinking of possible scenarios: His parents got it and forwarded it. They didn't get it. They got it and didn't forward it. They sent it on and he received it but wants nothing to do with it. He got it and he wants to answer it, but now he can't find it.
>   If a direct approach is possible, I think I'd like to lurch ahead with it. Perhaps I could write a letter to my son, if you would be able to send it in care of his parents' address.
> > Sincerely,
> > Margaret Moorman

February 2, 1995

Joyce called just as I was leaving the house to let me know that there would be a birth parents' meeting soon and that she would call to let me know the date. We talked for a while. She was packing for a trip to see her son and his adoptive parents in the Midwest. I told her I was about to jump out of my skin, waiting to hear from Winnicott. I told her that if it weren't two thousand dollars, I would hire a searcher to find him for me.

"Just a second," she said, putting down the phone. Waiting, I took a pen and doodled on the front page of yesterday's *Times*.

Joyce came back to the phone. "You can try this number. I think she's probably two thousand, though."

I scrawled a name and number in the margin of the front page, wondering if I'd remember to tear it off and save it before throwing out the papers. I didn't tear it off right away.

For the rest of the day, whenever I passed the newspaper on the table, I saw my handwriting out of the corner of my eye. Just before

I went to bed, I looked at it again. Then I shook my head at my own ambivalence, tore it off, and put it on top of a folder of clippings.

February 3, 1995

I took Laura to school, came home, got down to work writing, and made progress. When I looked at my watch it was lunchtime. I went to the kitchen to make myself something to eat, but when I got there I noticed I was carrying the torn scrap of newsprint. What the hell, I thought, maybe she'll do it for free.

The searcher answered on the first ring. Her voice had the hint of wariness I thought I'd discerned in that of Sue in Maryland who'd given me snippets of advice and encouragement, and also in a woman in Brooklyn whom I'd called to ask for the phone number that Joyce had eventually found for me.

There was a reason for their wariness. In 1993 a searcher named Sandra Musser had been convicted of fraud and conspiracy in a federal court. She claimed that her Musser Foundation had reunited about 500 adoptees children with their birth parents. The federal government claimed that she had violated the security and confidentiality of government records. The government had built its case in part on the testimony of an investigator who had pretended to be searching for a daughter given up for adoption. I had been having conversations with other birth mothers for nearly two years before they began suggesting I contact a searcher. It wasn't something they mentioned until they were sure they knew who I was and that my interest was wholly personal. Sandra Musser's conviction had sent a chill through the network.

According to most studies, open records are favored by ninety-five percent of birth parents and a solid majority of adoptees. More than half of adoptive parents are pro-open records. But those who are against openness are usually led by such vocal, powerful groups as the National Council for Adoption or NCFA, which recently lobbied heavily against a proposed open-records bill in New Jersey. The NCFA's William L. Pierce sent a letter to supporters in May of

1994 castigating the New Jersey bill and asking for funds to correct a $165,000 shortfall in their budget. By contrast, the Adoptees Political Action Committee, devoted to establishing voluntary triad registries and opening sealed records to adults, took in $1,448.40 in dues and contributions in 1994. They ended the year with assets of $100.54.

Many families call clandestine searches the underground railway to freedom. So long as groups like the NCFA fight open-records laws, people will do what they can—even break the law—to find their biological kin.

I had a long conversation with the searcher, a birth mother who had been a resident at the Florence Crittenden Home and Hospital in the early sixties. She was the one who told me it had been a good place to relax, think about your situation away from parents' "looks," and make your decision. "Contrary to what you hear from some birth mothers," she said, "we did have a choice, hard as it was."

It was the first time I'd heard another birth mother express the same sense of responsibility I'd always felt. It was refreshing to hear, even though my own perspective had changed. Now I wondered if my decision to give away my child had been shaped by pressures I had not understood and was incapable of resisting.

I made every indirect plea for financial aid that I could think of, but when the searcher found out Winnicott was my agency, she told me that it was a good place and that I should work with Marjorie Lane. "It's hard to search in D.C.," she said. "Really hard."

"Winnicott. . . ," she said musingly. "That was always an upper-crust agency." I had a flashback of my white cotton gloves, my mother's linen dresses, my heels, my flats.

"You've got to give it some time—say, six months—because, listen, you've been thinking about this for months, right?" I didn't have the nerve to tell her *years*. "But how long have these people had to form their response? They may be carefully working on their letter. Do you know anything about them?"

I told her about the Winnicott Christmas parties and his adopted sister—"That's good," she said—but that I didn't remember if the letter went to them or to my son in care of their address. I tried to reconstruct Marjorie Lane's description of the letter she sent.

"That's lovely," she said. "It's hard for most birth mothers to remember that there are other people's feelings involved here. I think that's a wonderful way to start."

I was surprised that this woman, whose business was finding birth families, was so concerned for the adoptive parents, but I was glad she was. Her attitude mirrored my feelings, if not my sense of urgency. Talking with her, I could see that waiting six months was what came next.

February 27, 1995

He *is* alive. That I can say with certainty.

I called Marjorie Lane again today. My gratitude for this woman would be boundless in a perfect world, where adoption records were open to all adults. She had written another letter to his parents, to confirm that my son received her letter, and she received a fax in return from his mother, saying that it had been forwarded to him.

Sometimes it takes a long time to digest the fact that a birth parent has made contact, Lane suggested gently. She said that was especially true when the adoption took place so long ago, when people more or less expected that they would never hear from the birth mother.

I said that although what she had achieved for me may seem like small change to her, it was of enormous importance to me, since I had never known even that he was alive.

Then she mentioned "the letter you got from us in 1991."

I racked my memory. Had I contacted Winnicott in 1991? Surely not. I was overwhelmed by Laura's ear infections the whole year. I was sleepless that year, and I remember I had to correct the galleys of *My Sister's Keeper* through tears of sheer fatigue. Why would I have called Winnicott? I told Lane I had no idea what she was talking about.

She began to describe a letter, but I interrupted her.

"What address was it sent to?"

The address was my old one, but badly garbled. Probably someone, somewhere in New York, had received it and had tossed it out, rather than taking the trouble of returning it to the post office, where it could have been returned to Winnicott, signalling them to check my address.

Winnicott had sent the 1991 letter in response to my 1987 call after my mother's death. There was a glancing apology for the delay. Not the *long* delay—nothing about the indecently attenuated interval of *four years*.

In that 1991 letter, Winnicott referred to a 1985 Christmas letter from my son's parents to the agency. Contrary to my original assumption that I was entitled to nothing, here was a luxurious array of facts, each one more astonishing than the last, and all openly supplied by my son's adoptive parents. My birth son was in school at a large university, where he had, on his own initiative, applied for and received a full Army ROTC scholarship. He had volunteered for a special "commando" unit. His parents described him and his younger adopted sister as "considerate and interesting people . . . nice people." (I loved them for that.) He was becoming fluent in German, a language I cannot begin to mimic or retain, but which his birth father knew. He was planning to take enough courses for both a bachelor's and a master's degree.

I blinked. "Was he adopted into a military family?" I asked.

No, Lane said. His father was an administrator involved in resource development and his mother was director of development at the private school his sister was then attending.

I remembered Linda Cannon Burgess's insistence on the issue of genetic heritage. I also had a clear memory of an adoptee who sued Geraldo Rivera for invasion of privacy after Rivera reunited him with his birth mother on national television. The adoptee was an actor; his birth mother and birth father were actors. His adoptive parents, whom he loved and revered, were interviewed by *People* magazine, and their words had rung in my ears: "It was a thrill to watch him grow, but he was so different from the rest of us."

It took me a while to speak. "You know who my birth son

takes after, don't you?" I asked, giddily assuming that Lane had memorized my file.

She said she didn't.

"His paternal grandfather, a navy captain." I felt a helpless urge to laugh, so I did.

Lane may have thought I was hysterical. She tried to assure me that he must take after me in *some* ways. She was comforting me, but I didn't need comforting. I was thrilled, at first. Here was a young man who knew what he wanted.

I laughed again. "Nope," I said delightedly. "Missed the mix altogether."

I felt light. It seemed all right, now, that I might never know this commando, and it seemed even more right that I had not reared him. It might have gone against his childish grain—to say nothing of his father's and grandfather's—if I had strollered him to anti-war protests in the late sixties.

I mentioned to Lane that I'd heard that men searched less frequently than women, and she agreed that in her experience that was true. And then I said something affectionately disparaging about thirty-year-old men in particular.

"Yes," she laughed. "He may have to chew on this for . . . ten or fifteen years."

I liked this Marjorie Lane.

To say nothing of his parents. Thank you, his parents. You were kind to write that holiday letter.

Harvey was thrilled, too. To him my son sounded like a person in charge of his life, "independent-minded, purposeful, living a useful life." I wondered and wondered. Was he still in the army? Was he married? Did he have children? Did he vote? Was he a Democrat or a Republican? I began to feel that nothing short of a reunion would do forever. It was already ten years since the information I now had about him was current. If Winnicott had answered my 1987 telephone call in a timely manner, I would have known these facts for eight years, now. They were fresh and exciting only because I'd just learned them, but a lot could happen in a decade. People changed in their twenties. They grew up. What had that process been like for him?

It did not occur to me, as it did to Joyce Bahr, some months later, that he might have been told that his birth father was in the navy, for that's where Dan was when I wrote my autobiography for Winnicott, and that would be a bit of information the adoptive parents might have been able to pass along to him as he was growing up. It saddened me, thinking that he might have been trying to connect with his birth father. I didn't want him to feel the need for that. I didn't want him to feel any longing that could not be satisfied. I wanted my child spared the pain that was so familiar to me. It was much more comfortable for me to think of him as natural commando material. I wanted to think of him as someone with whom I might not naturally connect, because then it was less painful, at least momentarily, to acknowledge that we might never meet.

Thinking of my son as a commando, I expected to feel reluctant to meet a young man who might take after Dan and Dan's father, but after a day or two I found that I wasn't. I was not afraid of this young man at all. I was not fifteen, sixteen, seventeen any more. I was a woman of forty-seven. Old enough to be his mother.

So a week later I wrote yet again to Winnicott.

> Dear Marjorie Lane: March 14, 1995
> Thank you for sending me the 1991 letter. I have to say it is somewhat shocking to me that it took Winnicott four years to form an answer to my telephone call of 1987. It would have saved me much worry . . . but better late than never.
> I know that when we spoke you said that the ball was in his court, but I want to try to persuade you to do more. First I wondered if you would forward a letter to him from me. I would be happy to have you look it over.
> Also, I have been troubled by the thought that since your tactful letter to him asked only for updated information he may feel that I am only curious and not that I am interested in a reunion. I do want a reunion, and I would be grateful if you could let him know.
> Can you give me any more facts about him? The region—

Northeast, Middle Atlantic, South, etc.—where he went to college? The state where he went to college?

Thank you again for your help. You have changed my perception of Winnicott. You've given me much peace of mind. I appreciate it.

Sincerely,

Then I tore up the letter and dialed her number.

Apparently there is nothing more that Winnicott will do for me. However, if I were to petition the D.C. court, there is a good chance the file would be opened.

Marjorie Lane gave me the name of an attorney in Washington who could petition the court to open my file. She expressed her understanding of my frustration. She said that it was a good sign that his parents had not called her to demand to know what was in the letter. To her, it meant that they "weren't paranoid." As usual, I took her assurances at face value.

I called the attorney and explained my situation. He quoted an estimated fee of $1,500.

An adoptive parent himself, he told me that he felt the mental illness in my family was something about which my son ought to know. He felt it was important to pass the information along to him, even though it was potentially frightening. He also said something that has bothered me ever after. He sighed and said that it was entirely possible—even likely—that my son's parents had not forwarded Winnicott's letter. "I've known a lot of adoptive parents," he said, "and it's a sad fact that most of them are frightened of any contact with birth parents." He could tell that this thought was yet another blow to me, and he gently apologized.

It was an unexpected blow, especially from an adoptive parent.

Dear Marjorie Lane: April 25, 1995
Thank you again for your conversation the last time we talked. I always appreciate your kindness.

Would it be possible for me to know two things: 1) My birth son's first name, and 2) whether his family still lived in the

D.C. area when he graduated from high school, which would have been in 1983, I believe.

Also, could you send me the name of that attorney again? (I put it in a safe place.) I spoke with him, and he said he felt that it was important for my son to know about the mental illness in my family, whether or not I want to open a dialogue with that painful information. He estimated his fee at about $1,500. I keep wondering, what if I were indigent and, say, carried the gene for cystic fibrosis? Would I be unable to pass that information along to a young man of childbearing age? Can you spell out Winnicott's policy for me? I feel sure I'm missing something. The $1,500 is not impossible for me, but it is daunting.

Thank you, and wishing you the very best, as always—
Sincerely yours,
Margaret Moorman

The New Yorker article on Cara Clausen was in the March 22, 1993, issue. Now, two slow, interesting, revelatory years later, it is spring again.

Last night I went to another Manhattan Birthparents Group meeting, where I brought Joyce and the others up to date on my progress. When I mentioned the 1985 letter from my son's parents in which his mother described her children as "considerate and interesting people . . . nice people," we all had to hold back tears.

Another birth mother spoke after me. "I think you're right about his parents," she said. "At least, his mother sounds great. And I think she wrote that letter to *you*. If she were just writing to the agency, she wouldn't write like that. She sounds really kind."

This woman was in close touch with her daughter and had been for many years. Her daughter's parents had been completely open from the start, sending pictures and letters to their child's birth mother all along. At first the correspondence went through the attorney who had handled the adoption, but as he aged, the birth mother became worried that he might die and that she would have no way to reach her daughter. "I went in one day to his office and said, 'Enough! I want their address! And I want you to give them mine!'

The lawyer sent a letter and they wrote back right away giving me their name and address. That's the kind of people they are!"

Others in the room were more skeptical. One had a son with whom she was in frequent contact. He still lived in his adoptive parents' home, even though he was recently married. His adoptive mother insisted she had given birth to him, even though as a young child he had found his adoption papers in a drawer and confronted her with them. "Oh, those are someone else's papers," she told him.

The birth mother felt caught in the middle, for the son could not bring himself to tell his adoptive mother that he had an ongoing relationship with his birth mother. Whispered telephone calls and secret meetings made the clandestine relationship difficult. The birth mother was sick of secrecy, and she was an open-records advocate. "I go along with this because my relationship with my son is more important to me than my own comfort," she said. She felt that if she pressed him—if she "outed" him in any way—it would destroy their rapprochement. This birth mother was one who did not buy the analysis that my son's mother was writing to me. To her, such thoughtful honesty was unimaginable.

Another woman who had found her daughter fifteen years earlier was equally doubtful. "My daughter's adoptive mother has had one and a half decades to get used to the idea that her daughter has another mother, too," she said, "But she still refuses to meet me. Let's face it. Most adoptive parents would be happier if we had died during childbirth."

Linda Cannon Burgess wrote, "The problem is not adoption itself but rather the way in which social institutions and individual adopters handle the situation."

I am going on with my education. I am a female, left-leaning liberal Democrat who went to college in the late 'sixties. I should know by now—and know by heart—that the personal is the political. This week, the New York state legislature is meeting and voting. I just mailed off a half-dozen postcards demanding that the mentally ill not be forgotten or short-changed during the budget talks, because although our new, Republican governor promised during his campaign not to cut funds to the mentally ill, he appears to have changed his mind once he was in office.

Also before the legislature is Bill Number 2328, proposing that adoptees be able to receive their original birth certificates when they are twenty-one. I called two lawmakers to register, as a birth mother and a voter, my support of the bill.

Thinking about Bill Number 2328, I also wrote a letter to a reporter who had written sensitively on adult adoptees who searched for their birth parents. I told her that there are some who feel that the largest search organizations in New York state seem strangely lukewarm when it comes to lobbying in behalf of the pending open-records bill. There is talk that these groups are not fighting for the bill—and for the interests of their constituents—because sealed records are their bread and butter. That's what I have heard, among the buzz of the birth-mom bees, so I am passing it on, trying to do a little public relations for the anti-secrecy sector.

This is an interesting and complicated new world, for me, and I can see that entering the big pond of politics makes it a little bit easier for a small frog to come out from under. It was so much harder when I was the only one of me in the imagined wading pool of the neighborhood playground. I think I will be able to tell Laura about all this, when the time comes, beginning with Michelle's words about the teenage girl and going on to talk about choices and sadness. And I think I will be able to hold my head up, if I have the chance to speak about being a birth mother. I feel all right—*just* all right, but that is a lot better than I used to feel—about myself and my past.

Once upon a time, I thought of my story as only that, but now I see it in a number of other ways. I see my story as a plea for family planning, for reproductive responsibility. I agree with those who say that giving away a child is an act that carries consequences that are inescapable for most birth mothers. I agree with the American

Adoption Congress, which has set new standards for achieving "informed consent" for women who are contemplating giving up their children. Abandoning them, in the eyes of the court.

Marjorie Lane called back to say that Winnicott would forward a letter to my son about the mental illness in the family. (I didn't think to wonder, then, why it had taken almost a year to tell me.)

"Oh God," I said.

"I'm sure you'll find the right words," she assured me, with her usual kindness.

Weeks slipped by. Finally one day I just sat down and wrote to him, doing the best I could.

> Dear Birth Son,   July 27, 1995
>   It is impossible to know how to begin a letter like this, so I am going to just plunge ahead and hope that whatever I say will strike the right chord in you.
>   I know very little about you, but your parents kindly and thoughtfully sent Winnicott information over the years that has been reassuring to me. The last I received was from 1985, when you were in college, in Army ROTC, and studying history and German. I hope you are well—and much more.
>   I won't try to fill in the years here, but perhaps you will want to know that your birth father and I did not marry. When I knew him he was ethical, smart, and capable. He was also only seventeen, so I am sure there is much more to him than I could tell you. His father was a navy captain—I thought of that when I learned you were in ROTC.
>   I am married to a painter who will be a visiting artist at American University in the fall. He has a daughter four years older than you, and she and her husband just had their first baby, our first grandchild. We also have a daughter, Laura, who will turn six in August. (We are fairly elderly as the parents of first-graders go, but in New York, where we live, there are a number of others like us.) I am taking the liberty of enclosing a picture of Laura. We have a mixed family—stepchildren and half-siblings and former in-laws—and a lot of affection going all around.
>   I would like very much to hear from you—and I would like to meet. I realize that you may not wish to see me, or to corre-

spond. Could you communicate that through Winnicott, if that is how you feel?

I have been trying to sort out my thoughts about you and about my experience as a birth mother, and I've been writing about it all, since that is what I do. My first book was about my sister, Sally, who has been ill since her teens, and how her illness affected our family over the years. She is now diagnosed as having bipolar illness (manic depression). She is fifty-four and doing well. I am very proud of her, as her life has been difficult and she has really triumphed over this disease. I was told by a Winnicott representative that I may pass this information along to you, as it is potentially medically significant, but I have been reluctant, knowing that mental illness can be frightening. I used to find it frightening myself, until I learned more about it. For many years I worried that I might become ill, too, and also worried about whether the illness could be inherited by my children. As you may be able to tell, those worries are behind me, and I hope you will take my assurances to heart that you shouldn't spend much time with them either. I am using this medical information somewhat disingenuously—while it may be of use to you, it is also the only way I am able to reach out to you. Please forgive me.

My second book was an illustrated one, for children—a lot more fun than the first, especially the pictures. If you would like either book, I would be happy to send it to you.

This has become too long, so I will close.

I wrote my name, address, and telephone number.

I sent the letter to Winnicott with a note asking them to let me know if they needed to edit it. I didn't hear back from them, and I am afraid that for a few months I assumed my letter was sitting in a pile on Marjorie Lane's desk. One would think that by now I would have stopped assuming anything, but I found I could not shake the feeling that I would have to prod Winnicott to make any move on my behalf.

That was not true, as I found when I summoned the courage to call Marjorie Lane again, toward the end of the year, near the holidays. She told me that Winnicott had obtained my birth son's address from his parents and written to him to let him know there was a letter from me at the agency that contained medical information. He had called Winnicott to say that he would like to receive it. They had sent it on to him within a few weeks of receiving it from me. While their methods seem a bit stiff to me, Winnicott is now largely redeemed in my eyes. Considering their policies, they easily might have demanded a less open letter from me. They didn't. Through Winnicott, I was able to communicate with my son.

At first I was hurt that he hadn't called or written. Marjorie Lane found several ways to tell me that this was especially common among young men. She suggested that if he married his wife might be the one to encourage him to respond. I hung up feeling vaguely regretful that I had told him so much about myself. I have heard birth mothers tell others that it is a mistake to say too much in a letter. It may satisfy the curiosity of the other person, who then may feel no need for anything further. But I felt I had to tell him the good parts, given the fact that I had some potentially depressing information for him. I wanted to balance that with the happiness of our lives, in which he was welcome to share.

It was only a matter of minutes, however, before I realized that at least he hadn't told Winnicott he did not want to communicate with me. He hadn't closed that door. (I did not realize that he would be able to reach me only through Winnicott. They had crossed out my name, address, and telephone number.)

And it had been only a couple of months. God willing, I had years to wait, and Laura much longer. I forgot to ask if they sent him the picture of her. I was careful, in my letter, not to call Laura his sister. He had a sister, already. But perhaps he would feel some kinship with Laura. I hoped so.

Some friends suggested that he could be trying to resolve old feelings of anger or abandonment before he got in touch. Others said it was possible he was worried that it would hurt his adoptive parents if he were to get in touch with me.

For the most part, I felt peaceful. There was the usual sense of accomplishment that I've known after each step forward, but this time there was also something much more important to me: I felt relieved, immensely relieved, to be certain that this man, this child of mine, finally knew that I cared about him.

At least *I* knew I cared about him, whoever he was, whoever he resembled, whoever his parents had brought him up to be, whoever he had chosen to become. He was my kin, and I was his, and that would be true forever.

Three days after I spoke with Marjorie Lane, she left a message on my answering machine: "I just wanted to let you know that we received something and that I've put it in the mail for you." When I called back, she had left for the day.

The hives didn't last all night this time. They were gone by midnight, and I slept well. I knew nothing could arrive overnight, but I began casting prayerful glances at the mailbox whenever I passed it.

Another night, and then a long December day on which the mail was, of course, late.

And then, toward evening, the letter.

The letter.

How can I describe it, and the effect it had on me? If I were writing fiction, and I wanted to compose a letter at the end of the book that would fill the birth mother's heart with love, her soul with peace, and give her the kind of pleasure and joy that can usually be had only in the sort of sentimental novels I wouldn't trouble to read, because they are too good to be true, I would have to come up with something like the generous, open, informative letter I received from my birth son.

He is a happy-sounding, busy young man with a full life, a family life, and a letter-writing style that is . . . familiar to me. Everything about him is familiar. There is a slight (he is young) elegiacal quality to his observations. He lives in my grandmother's hometown, far from where he was adopted. He went to graduate school at the same university as a cousin of mine, in the town where another relative, now in her eighties, has lived for more than half a century. He sent a picture. He looks like me. He looks very much like me.

He is an appreciative, affectionate son. His stories about his childhood are the stories of a treasured child. If, before, I was confident about his parents, now I love them. I hope I can take his mother's hands in mine someday.

He doesn't want to meet, for now. He thinks it might cause his mother to worry. He apologized for disappointing me. It is true that I want to meet him, but five days later, I still feel no disappointment. There may not be room, I am so stuffed with relief and happiness. For nearly two days I was euphoric, wearing the old foolish grin as I floated around the house. I remembered the last time, when the stick turned pink, and I felt as if my son had just been born. This time, I was as happy as I had been with Laura. I had never expected this—to feel this kind of love.

As the euphoria began to wear off, I slept. All day, all night, when I could. Exhausted. Just today I've recovered part of my strength, but I'm woozy, as if I have just woken up from a long, complicated dream. I have a dozen new gray hairs, and that's just in front, where I can see them.

I keep waiting to feel the obvious thing—to wish that I had kept him. Of course, I do wish that. I have always wished it. But his letter seems to have gently closed the door on the past, on the old regrets, even on the pain. Gone. Gone! Here is the present, instead, full of life, and the future, full of promise. The morning after the letter came, Harvey sat up in bed when the alarm went off, opened his eyes wide, smiled, and called out, "Day One!"

We are happy. Life after letter. Day five, A.L. As I looked at the letter, held the letter, touched the letter, quoted from the letter, looked for the right safe place to put the letter, Harvey murmured, "Just don't try to bronze it."

I close my eyes and say the prayer of thanks that I have wanted to say for years. Thank you, God, for all your blessings. Thank you for the daughter; thank you for the son.